Privatization and Privilege
in Education

Privatization and Privilege in Education

Geoffrey Walford

R

ROUTLEDGE
London and New York

First published 1990
by Routledge
11 New Fetter Lane, London EC4P 4EE

Simultaneously published in the USA and Canada
by Routledge
a division of Routledge, Chapman and Hall, Inc.
29 West 35th Street, New York, NY 10001
© 1990 Geoffrey Walford

Phototypeset in 10pt Times by
Mews Photosetting, Beckenham, Kent
Printed and bound in Great Britain by
Biddles Ltd, Guildford and King's Lynn

British Library Cataloguing in Publication Data

Walford, Geoffrey
   Privatization and privilege in education.
   1. Great Britain. Private education
   I. Title
   379.3

   0-415-04247-X
   0-415-04248-8 (pbk)

Contents

List of tables

Acknowledgements

Chapter four contains some material by the author which has previously been published in the following articles: 'How dependent is the independent sector?', *Oxford Review of Education* 13, 3 (1987) 275–96; 'The privatisation of British higher education', *European Journal of Education* 23, 1/2 (1988) 47–64. We are most grateful to the publishers for their permission to use this material.

Private schools have long been a major source of perpetuated division and the demarcation of privilege, status, esteem, power, opportunity and expectation that go with it. Private schools are not 'incidental' to the class system. They are the very cement in the wall that divides British society. The existence of private schooling with all its increments of status and complementary paraphernalia of quaint uniforms and traditions, language and accents is amongst the most offensive means of perpetually imposing those divisions.

[Neil Kinnock, Labour Party press release, 13 July 1981]

Independent schools are an important part of our school system. Their diversity and existence valuably increase the choice available to parents. We welcome the continuing contribution of a healthy independent sector towards the development of tomorrow's adult citizens.

Question. Are independent schools 'divisive'?

Certainly not. People want variety and freedom to choose in all areas of life. In the sphere of education, parents choose particular schools for many different reasons. The right to exercise parental choice is a key component of a free society.

[Kenneth Baker, in an interview with David Woodhead,
ISIS News, spring 1987]

Introduction

Politicians, policy-makers, and the general public tend to have strong opinions about private schools. They are often either firmly in favour of them or equally firmly against, with little room for discussion or compromise. What debate that occurs is usually conducted more in terms of polemic than of rational argument, and a detailed knowledge about private schools is often lacking. This scantiness of knowledge about private education is perhaps understandable, for media coverage of the subject largely concentrates on the elite part of the sector. In many people's minds the private schools have thus become associated, and perhaps synonymous with, the public schools. Schools such as Eton, Harrow, and Winchester come to mind, each with its own quaint uniforms and traditions, language and accents. Sportsmen may also remember Rugby, while Gordonstoun's name might well be recognized by avid followers of royalty. For girls, Benenden, Roedean, and Cheltenham Ladies' number among the best known schools.

While such elite schools may be important in terms of the reproduction and maintenance of positions of power and privilege (and even here the nature of the link is not as obvious as it might seem), they are far from being representative of the wide variety of schools within the private sector. In 1987 there were about 2,400 independent or private schools in Great Britain. They educated more than 560,000 children, just over 7 per cent of school-age pupils, and about 18 per cent of those in school sixth forms. Within this large number of schools there is considerable variability which is often hidden by a concentration on the activity of the major schools only. Thus, while about 25 per cent of those at university were educated at private schools, as were nearly half the undergraduates at Oxford and Cambridge Universities, a private school education is far from being an automatic entry into university. The vast majority of privately educated university entrants come from the elite schools and not the private sector as a whole, so to concentrate study on these major schools only can lead to a misunderstanding of the private sector, and the way it relates to the maintained sector. For the private sector is characterized by its diversity as much as its elitism, and in this book it is hoped to present a clear picture of the nature and extent of the whole private sector of British schooling.

Such a clarification is a first and necessary step towards a greater understanding of the blurring of the boundaries that is currently occurring between the private and state maintained sectors, which is the direct result of government policy in promoting the privatization of education. Since coming to power in 1979 the Conservative government has encouraged private education both financially and ideologically. It has also made major changes to the maintained sector, especially through the 1988 Education Reform Act, which attempted to make state schools more like those in the private sector. The city technology college, for example, is an entirely new form of private school funded jointly by industry and government, while grant maintained schools give a greater degree of independence to schools previously under local education authority or Church control. This book examines these recent changes within the educational system, but does so through an examination of the private sector first. This somewhat unusual concentration on the private sector sheds considerable light on the ideological basis of the many recent changes in the maintained sector, and enables us to understand what sort of utopia the government has in mind for education in Britain.

The first chapter of the book thus describes the nature and diversity of the private sector, while the second gives a description of the historical development of maintained schools in relation to the private sector. It also discusses the changing positions of the major political parties. Those readers who already have a good understanding of the private sector may be tempted to skip these chapters, but the information here is vital to a full understanding of later chapters.

Chapter three examines the nature and extent of the privileges which may be obtained for children at some of these private schools. It charts the inequalities in provision and outcomes that parents are able to purchase for their offspring.

Chapter four introduces the concept of privatization, and shows that what is occurring in education is very similar to the privatization processes being enforced in health and welfare services. The way in which the 1988 Education Reform Act builds upon earlier privatization processes and introduces new elements is the topic of chapter five.

The final chapter puts forward some objections to private schools and to privatization, and examines the balance between choice and freedom for individuals and the structured inequality which is perceived to be the inevitable accompaniment. It describes the nature of the educational system which will result if the privatization process is allowed to come to completion, and makes proposals for action towards a more just and equitable future.

Chapter one

Private schools

What is a private school?

The first step in mapping and understanding the private sector is to try to answer the deceptively simple question of definition. In Britain the term 'private school' is not the one most commonly used, and the term 'independent school' now has a far greater prominence. 'Independent' is also now the term used by the Department of Education and Science, which defines an independent school as one providing education for five or more school-age children and not being maintained by the state. The term 'private' has been used in this book for three reasons. First, it is the term most used in practically every other country for schools other than those provided and financed by the state (Walford, 1989). Second, as will be shown in chapter four, 'independent' is far from being a satisfactory description of the relationship between the state and these schools, for in recent years they have become increasingly dependent upon government financial and ideological support. Third, the distinction between schools classified as independent and those classified as state maintained is being blurred as a result of recent government education policy. One of the main aims of this book is to argue that this process is best understood as an example of privatization.

The choice of terminology used to describe these schools is far from being a neutral decision. Each term is ideologically loaded, none more so than the now less frequently used 'public school'. There is no legal or even agreed definition of what a public school is. The term is a contested accolade, and even its origin is in dispute. Some argue that it is derived from the fact that many of the ancient schools established in the fourteenth, fifteenth, and sixteenth centuries were originally founded to provide free education for the poor. However, there is a debate about how poor the children were expected to be, and in several cases it may mean no more than 'not exceedingly rich' (Walford, 1986a: 6). Other writers argue that these schools became known as public in that they replaced the private tutors of the aristocratic household. Another

3

explanation is that the statutes of some schools allowed a certain number of fee-paying pupils (who were thus from the public, if only from a limited range of it) as well as those scholars on the foundation. Finally, some writers argue that public schools are so called because they are open to pupils from all over the country and not just from the local neighbourhood.

The Clarendon Commission of 1861, which investigated the horrendous state into which some of the endowed schools had by then fallen, acted as a marker defining nine schools as 'Great or Public Schools'. These were Charterhouse, Eton, Harrow, Merchant Taylors', Rugby, St Paul's, Shrewsbury, Westminster, and Winchester. Merchant Taylors' and St Paul's were day schools. Honey (1977) claims that the use of the term gradually spread as other schools were recognized as equals by schools from within the nine. Regular sports fixtures, especially in cricket, were a key part in this acceptance of status. By the 1960s membership of the Headmasters' Conference was usually taken as indicating that a school might call itself a public school if it wished. But, by that time, some schools were becoming wary of using the term, for it carried with it associations of elitism and privilege at a time when these were unfashionable.

As Rae (1981) argues, 'that the term "public school" should be obsolescent is something of a triumph for the schools' public relations . . . Few British people could be expected to rally to the defence of the public schools, but independence was a wider and much more fundamental issue.' The major schools joined with the majority of the other private-sector schools to present an image of 'independence', which brought into the debate questions of freedom of choice and individual liberty. The Independent Schools Information Service (ISIS) and the Independent Schools Joint Council (ISJC) were formed to present the views of the whole sector to the public, to politicians and to policymakers, and both bodies have been very successful.

Some critics have wished to use other terms to describe the schools, such as 'fee-paying' or 'commercial' (Halsey, 1981), which stress the market basis of these schools, but the term 'private' has increasingly come to be the most appropriate one to describe the sector. One of the major features of the three Thatcher governments has been the privatization of a whole host of companies and welfare services formerly in the hands of the state. In the government's eyes 'private' has come to be associated with greater individual choice and freedom, innovation, and efficiency. Yet, at the same time, the political left have come to associate 'private' and 'privatization' with the inequality, exploitation, and individualistic competitiveness which they perceive the government's policies promote. Thus, while the official nomenclature is in terms of independent schools, the 'private' designation would appear to be the most appropriate to use here.

Diversity within the private sector

The private education sector is highly diverse. At the macro descriptive level there are a growing number of schools which are co-educational, while some schools still cater for boys only and others for girls only. In contrast to what may be the usual assumption, some two-thirds of the schools are for day pupils only, and most of those with accommodation for boarders also accept day pupils. An equally fundamental distinction concerns the age range of pupils in the schools. While there is a growth in the number of schools establishing facilities to cater for all school-age pupils, most schools provide for a more limited range, although the ages of transfer do not always coincide with the primary/secondary division in the state maintained sector. As might be expected, the geographical distribution of schools is very uneven, there being far more schools in the south than in the north of England, and a concentration of schools in urban areas.

Information on such obvious variables is valuable, but the most fruitful way of describing the diversity of the sector is through a consideration of the various organizations of which the schools are members. Both historically and currently, the most important of these organizations is the Headmasters' Conference.

The Headmasters' Conference

The Headmasters' Conference has its origin in Edward Thring's proposal in 1869 for a regular meeting of headmasters of major endowed schools, who had been meeting irregularly before then, to develop a defence against the perceived threat to the independence of the endowed schools contained in the Endowed Schools (No. 2) Bill (Leinster-Mackay, 1987). Thirty-seven headmasters were invited to the first meeting, but only twelve attended. The following year, however, thirty-four Heads turned up, including the Heads from the seven public schools which had been defined and investigated by the Clarendon Commission. In 1871 a constitution was drawn up and it was resolved to establish an annual meeting of the headmasters of the 'Highest Schools', which included all schools of the 'First Grade', whether they were called public schools, endowed schools, proprietary schools, or colleges. In practice, the case for admission of a headmaster was judged by a committee on the basis of the number of boys in the school, the proportion who went on to university, and the degree of independence that the headmaster had in the running of the school. It was assumed at the start, and for many years after, that 'First Grade' schools were for boys only.

There were fifty schools with headmasters in membership of the HMC in 1871, rising to seventy-nine in 1886. After 1914 there was a limit of 150 members, which was raised to 200 in 1937 (Honey, 1977). By 1988 the nature and variety of the schools in membership had changed considerably from the early days. By that year there were 228 HMC schools (including 8 in the island of Ireland), with 149,000 pupils, including 23,000 girls. Only about 30 per cent of these pupils boarded. Even within this group of just over 200 schools there is considerable diversity. They range in size from about 310 at Mount St Mary's to nearly 1,300 at Eton. Some have histories dating back to the fifteenth century or earlier, some were founded in the mid-nineteenth century to educate the sons of the rising middle class who found their wealth in the rapid industrialization of the period, while others were founded in the 1920s just before the depression. Over seventy of the schools were at one time direct grant schools, most of which were for day pupils only and, as described in chapter three, only became fully independent again after the direct grant was phased out from 1975 onwards (Price, 1986). The average termly fees for all HMC schools in 1987/8 were £1,895 for full boarding and £784 for pupils in day-only schools (ISIS, 1988). At Stowe School termly fees were £2,355, and they were £2,331 at Winchester College. 'Extras' may be added to this.

While the ex-direct grant schools form one loose grouping within the HMC, the twenty-nine schools in membership of the Rugby or Eton Groups can be seen as another (Walford, 1986a). The Rugby Group of schools consists of seventeen of the major boarding schools. It was formed on an *ad hoc* basis in the 1960s to enable headmasters and senior masters at these schools to meet their opposite numbers in similar schools to discuss matters of common interest. The Eton Group started a little later and now has twelve schools but, unlike the Rugby Group, includes some schools where most of the pupils are not boarders. The list of twenty-nine schools includes Eton and Harrow, Westminster, Wellington and Winchester, and Radley, Repton, and Rugby. All but one of the twelve schools recognized by the Clarendon Commission as 'great or public schools' are included, and they can be usefully regarded as the 'market leaders'.

There is also great diversity in religious affiliation, which can have a major effect on the ethos of the school. Nearly all the 100 or so schools in HMC where all or most of the pupils board have a direct connection with one of the Christian denominations. Ten of the schools are Roman Catholic – Ampleforth and Downside, for example, being still run by English Benedictine monks. Eight have links with the Methodist Church, two are Quaker, and about sixty are associated with the Church of England. Historically, a number of the latter schools were established in order to transmit a specific tradition within the Anglican Church. Thus Dean Close emphasized the evangelical tradition, while the Woodard schools, such as Lancing and Bloxham, held to the Anglo-Catholic persuasion. These original links have not necessarily been maintained to the present day.

Until the 1960s all HMC schools were for boys only. Schools which were recognized as having a similar standing, but which were co-educational, had been excluded on the basis that they took girls as well as boys. However, when Marlborough College, one of the leading schools, started to admit girls into its sixth form, the HMC was forced to accept that it would have to change its policy. While Marlborough's reasons for introducing girls were not financial, this does appear to have been a reason for some other schools making the change. For Marlborough and the other major schools the advantage was that they were able to attract girls of high academic ability who could boost the academic standing of the school (Walford, 1983). Girls were also often seen as a civilizing influence on the boys, and for some schools provided a welcome extension to the potential market. Change has been rapid, and by 1988 about seventy HMC schools were fully co-educational, while another eighty admitted some girls at sixth-form level only. More than half the HMC schools thus now admit girls.

The traditional age range for the boarding schools in HMC has been 13–18, but many of the schools catering predominantly for day pupils take pupils from 11. This is particularly true of the ex-direct grant schools in membership, which formerly had very close links with the maintained sector. However, the distinction is not fixed and there has been a tendency in recent years for boarding schools to accept pupils at 11 as well as 13, often in a special lower school or linked preparatory school.

The majority of sociological research and educational writing about private education has actually been concerned with just the HMC schools, rather than the full range. They have often been taken as synonymous with the 'public' schools. Though there are some very good reasons for this focus, it has meant that those outside the system, including politicians, have often received a distorted vision of the nature of private schooling. A further problem is that most of the sociological work is now out of date, as the major schools have changed considerably in the last few decades. Among the most important historical and educational studies are those by Bamford (1967), Chandos (1984), Dancy (1966), Gathorne-Hardy (1977), Honey (1977), MacDonald Fraser (1977), Mack (1941), Ogilvie (1957), Rae (1981), and Simon and Bradley (1975). The major sociological studies are Wakeford (1969), Walford (1986a), Weinberg (1967), and Wilkinson (1964). A major sociological study of boarding schools, which emphasized the HMC schools, was conducted by Lambert and co-workers in the late 1960s (Lambert, 1966; Lambert and Millham, 1968; Lambert *et al.*, 1968; Lambert, 1975). As will be shown in chapter three, Lambert's early work influenced the findings of the Public Schools Commission, which reported in 1968.

The Girls' Schools Association

For girls' private schools the organization which is usually taken as somewhat analogous to the HMC is the Girls' Schools Association (GSA) and the linked Governing Bodies of Girls' Schools Association (GBGSA). Interestingly, the organization which was originally most closely analogous to the HMC, the Association of Headmistresses, founded by Frances Mary Buss in 1874, broadened its membership to include all headmistresses as the maintained sector developed. The improvement of girls' education as a whole was seen as more important than any maintenance of exclusiveness (Price and Glenday, 1974). The Girls' Schools Association, on the other hand, is restricted to headmistresses of private schools.

In 1988 there were 259 schools in membership of the GSA/GBGSA, with a considerable range in terms of size, academic emphasis, geography, religious affiliation, and so on. One area where there is less diversity than the HMC schools is in terms of the date of foundation of the schools, for the earliest date from the middle of the nineteenth century. The development of girls' private secondary schools must be seen in the context of growing female emancipation through that century, and the work of a small number of educational pioneers. In 1850 the North London Collegiate School began under the headship of Frances Mary Buss, and with the collaboration of her parents and brothers. She created a school which became a model for girls' education and helped to inspire the Girls' Public Day School Company (later Trust), which in 1988 controlled twenty-four secondary schools (Reynolds, 1950). In a similar way, Dorothea Beale developed Cheltenham Ladies' College when she became Head in 1858 of a school created some four years earlier. A third pioneer, Mary Eliza Porter, became the first headmistress of four major new schools between 1871 and 1880.

The major studies of girls' schools are now all rather dated, but include Ollerenshaw's (1967) study of GBGSA schools, and Wober's (1971) account of girls' boarding schools. This was part of the larger study of boarding schools conducted by Lambert and his colleagues. Sociological accounts are given by Delamont (1976a, b; 1984), who concentrates on interactionist perspectives, Okely (1978), whose work is semi-autobiographical, and the impressionistic work by Lamb and Pickthorne (1968).

Proportionally, fewer girls than boys board. Just 21 per cent of girls in GSA/GBGSA schools board, compared with 31 per cent of the boys in HMC schools. There are thus fewer schools with a full-boarding ethos, and the influence of the day schools, many of which were once direct grant schools, dominates the group. There is more variability in the age at which girls enter the schools. While a very few schools cater for

13–18, the same at the major HMC boarding schools, the vast majority have an intake at 11, with the possibility of also entering at 12 or 13. This means that the total age range catered for is rather large, and the controls that are necessary for 11-year-olds may make the ethos of the school somewhat unattractive to 18-year-olds. Many of those girls who transfer to HMC schools for their sixth-form years do so in part because they believe that they will enter a more mature atmosphere (Walford, 1986a: 162).

Some of the schools within the GSA/GBGSA have tried to take in boys, in a similar way to that of HMC schools accepting girls, but fewer schools have tried, and they have been far less successful. Whereas about 15 per cent of pupils in HMC schools are girls, less than 2 per cent of pupils in GSA/GBGSA schools are boys. In 1988 only twenty-nine of these boys were boarders. The average termly fees for these schools are somewhat lower than those for HMC schools, being £1,701 for full boarding and £732 for pupils in day schools (ISIS, 1988), but rise to £2,150 at Benenden, and £2,290 at Roedean.

Preparatory schools

Some HMC schools and GSA/GBGSA schools have their own preparatory departments and schools attached, so that about 8 per cent of HMC pupils are actually aged 10 or below, as are some 22 per cent of pupils in GSA/GBGSA schools. However, the majority of private-school pupils below 11 are in separate preparatory schools. The moves towards co-education for younger children have been so substantial that the two organizations formerly representing the main schools in the sector have now combined. Until 1981 the Incorporated Association of Preparatory Schools (IAPS) represented the headmasters of boys' and co-educational schools, while the much smaller Association of Head-mistresses of Preparatory Schools represented the headmistresses of girls' and co-educational schools. After amalgamation the new group took the IAPS name. There are now 556 schools in membership, including five in Ireland.

Until recently the history of the preparatory schools had been sadly neglected, and apart from accounts of individual schools (such as Batchelor, 1981, and Briggs, 1983) there was little which looked at the sector as a whole. This neglect has now been rectified by a major study by Leinster-Mackay (1984) which charts the emergence of preparatory schools during the nineteenth century from their precursors of the private classical schools and better dame preparatory schools of the preceding centuries. It was not until that time that the public schools ceased to take young boys and there gradually developed a group of schools designed specifically to prepare boys for entry to those schools. Leinster-Mackay argues that the oldest preparatory school in terms of date of foundation, irrespective of when it actually became a preparatory school, is the York Minster Song School, founded in 627. However, the two schools which have a claim to be the first schools to possess essential preparatory school characteristics are Twyford and Temple Grove, both of which had become preparatory before 1835. Thereafter there was a slow growth in the first half of the nineteenth century, an acceleration in the third quarter, and a rapid increase in the last quarter. The Clarendon Report of 1864 helped clarify the use of the term by recognizing the need for separate treatment of younger boys and by discussing the age of transfer between schools.

The Association of Preparatory Schools developed from a meeting in 1892 of a small number of headmasters of preparatory schools to discuss the weight and size of the cricket ball to be used by boys at their schools. Incorporation took place in 1923. Under the rules of the Association members may keep pupils until their fifteenth birthday, but the vast majority of pupils are under 14 years old. Boys usually leave their prep. schools at 13, but girls may leave to go to girls' senior schools at various ages from 11 to 13. The age of entry to the schools is also varied. Eight is the traditional age of entry, but an increasing number of prep. schools now have pre-prep. departments which take children from 5 or younger. This has been the case with many girls' preparatory schools for some years, but has increased markedly for boys' and co-educational schools as well. This extension into pre-prep. accounts for some of the rapid growth in pupil numbers in IAPS schools that has been recently experienced (about 3 per cent per year for the three years to 1988).

These schools are usually far smaller than the private senior schools, having fewer than 200 pupils on average. About 19 per cent of the pupils are full boarders and a further 3 per cent are weekly boarders, going home at weekends. The average termly fee in 1988 was £1,436 for full board and £710 for pupils in day schools, but the variation was considerable, with one school charging over £2,000 and another less than £400 for full board. Clearly the facilities on offer are likely to vary in a similar way.

Other schools

The schools in membership of the three associations already discussed account for 1,028 of the private schools in Great Britain and 363,000 of the pupils. Thus two-thirds of private pupils are in these schools. The other one-third are in an even wider range of schools than has been indicated so far. Some are in reputable schools in membership of some other smaller associations, discussed below, while others are in small private special schools. Others are in well known progressive schools, which promote different values from those of the recognized associations and thus do not wish to join. Others still are in small proprietary schools run for private profit, some of which may well be distinctly cheap and shady.

Forty-four of the boys' and co-educational senior schools are grouped together in the Society of Headmasters of Independent Schools (SHMIS), which was founded in 1961, mainly to represent the smaller schools. The average size of HMC schools in now over 650 pupils, whereas SHMIS schools usually have under 300 pupils. Some of the schools in this group are well known, such as Abbotsholme, founded in 1889 by Dr Cecil Reddie, or the Jewish Carmel College, with termly fees in the range £2,500–£2,950. It also includes Chetham's School of Music and the Purcell School for young musicians. Termly fees for boarding average at £1,788 for full board and £776 for pupils in day schools.

An indication of the general standing of the schools in this group is that they are listed in the *Public and Preparatory Schools Yearbook* for each year. The *Yearbook*, which has come to be regarded as the standard handbook to the major boys' and co-eductional schools, gives details of HMC, IAPS, and SHMIS schools.

A further association to consider is the Governing Bodies Association (GBA), which with the GBGSA has over 500 senior schools in membership. Most of the headmasters of these schools are usually members of the HMC or SHMIS and the headmistresses are members of the GSA. However, sixteen schools are only members of the GBA and are sometimes classified together as a group. The primary aim of the GBA is to act as an advisory body for the governors of members schools on educational and administrative matters, and as a co-ordinating organization for independent secondary schools. These sixteen schools cater for about 7,400 pupils, more than 70 per cent of whom are boys.

Finally, 264 schools are members of the Independent Schools' Association Incorporated (ISAI). This body was set up in 1895 as the Private Schools' Association but changed its name to ISAI in 1927, many years before 'Independent' became the favoured designation. The members are Heads of independent secondary schools. The majority of these schools are day schools and only 10 per cent of the pupils are boarders. The termly fees payable are considerably lower than those for the other groups considered so far, averaging £1,471 for full board and £592 for pupils in day schools. A crude indication of the academic standing of these schools is the fact that, while in 1988 there were 48,800 pupils in these schools, a total of only 473 pupils left in the previous year to go on to university or polytechnic degree courses. The HMC sector is about three times the size of ISAI, but the number leaving to go to university or polytechnic degree courses was thirty times as large. As discussed in chapter three, while such comparisons may be indicative

11

of the orientation of these schools, they do not give any guide to their effectiveness even in the very limited sense of getting pupils into higher education. The results obtained by any school are dependent upon the 'quality' of the pupil intake, and these schools are far less academically selective than the other schools so far discussed.

All the above associations are members of the Independent Schools Information Service (ISIS), which was established in 1972 to act as an information centre for the schools. Far more information is available about these schools than about the rest of the system. Indeed, it is ISIS Annual Census figures which usually feature in the press and other media reports about the private school sector, and it is often assumed that what occurs in ISIS schools can be taken as indicative of the whole of the British system. But, in fact, while ISIS schools contain about 80 per cent of the pupils in the private sector, it has only about half of all the private schools in membership. A further confusion is that thirteen of the ISIS schools are actually in Ireland, yet their figures are usually included with those of the other British schools in any discussion. In 1988 ISIS member associations accounted for 1,369 British private schools out of a total of about 2,500.

General information on the schools not linked with ISIS is difficult to find. The recent *Parents' Guide to Independent Schools* (1988) gives some help. It provides profiles of nearly 2,000 independent schools in the UK which were either 'recognized as efficient' by the DES up to the time when this practice ceased in April 1978, or which are members of the various independent schools' organizations. About ninety senior schools are listed without any association membership. Most of these are small Roman Catholic schools with about 200–300 pupils, predominantly girls, and run by nuns. Some of the other schools are simply small day schools charging low fees, and presumably having correspondingly poor facilities. The majority of these ninety schools only take pupils up to 16. The same *Parents' Guide* lists just over 200 preparatory schools which are not members of IAPS or any of the other recognized associations. Here, too, there are a good proportion of Roman Catholic schools, but there are also many inter- and non-denominational as well as Anglican schools. All of them are small.

There remain some several hundred private schools still to be accounted for, and it is within this collection of schools that the extent of the diversity of the sector is at its most evident. The majority of such schools are probably simply small local private schools which cater for the pre-prep. age group. It has been shown that prep. schools traditionally start at age 7, while compulsory schooling starts at 5. Where preparatory schools have their own pre-prep. departments – and an increasing number now do – these pupils are included in the numbers for the prep. school. But where a separate school exists just for pre-prep. neither the

Parents' Guide nor any ISIS publications list the schools. This pre-prep. area is actually one of the fastest areas of growth for the private sector as a whole.

But these pre-prep. schools only account for some of the 'missing' schools. Another group are private schools for children with special educational needs. Most of these take about fifty pupils and the fees are paid by the local education authority from which the child comes. Other special schools make provision for dyslexic children, or children with problems of hearing or sight. Special in a rather different sense is the internationally famous Summerhill, founded by A.S. Neill (1962), which became a blueprint for free schooling during the 1960s, and the somewhat similar Kilquhanity House School in Scotland, run by John Aitkenhead (1986). Both these schools are small, but Hamilton College, a co-educational day school in Strathclyde, now has nearly 900 pupils. Hamilton, which opened only in 1983, is housed in the buildings of a former college of education, the sale of which was the subject of considerable controversy at the time. It puts emphasis on biblically based evangelical Christianity and is part of a growing group of related schools.

Provision for religious diversity is a common justification for many of these schools. Evangelical Christianity is also the basis of a group of small schools established and run by Churches in the early 1980s some of which originally based their teaching on materials published by Accelerated Christian Education Inc. (PACE) of the United States. In 1985 there were about thirty such schools. They attracted media attention because of their ritualistic administration of corporal punishment, and several of the schools were inspected by HM inspectors in early 1985. The limited facilities and narrow curriculum were heavily criticized in the published reports, but similar schools still exist, including one in Hertfordshire with over 100 pupils (Wallace, 1988).

Other religious-based schools also thrive. The John Loughborough School in Tottenham, for example, is an all-black Seventh Day Adventist secondary school for about 300 pupils. There is a strong academic emphasis, and examination successes are high. Also thriving are several Jewish schools and Muslim schools, some of which have tried for years to become part of the maintained sector through voluntary aided status. The increased internationalism of business has meant that whole families from other nations now visit for long periods, but do not wish their children to be educated within the British system. Thus there are now Japanese schools in London and Milton Keynes, and several American schools scattered throughout the country. There is a European school at Culham, associated with the European JET Project. A number of these schools exist to promote a particular philosophy of schooling, such as those in the 'small school' movement (Winsor, 1987). Even Warlingham Park School, established by Stuart Sexton, former political adviser to

Sir Keith Joseph, as a private technology primary school, is among this collection of schools without membership of any of the major associations.

This partial survey gives an indication of the extent of diversity of provision within only the private school sector. While this book is predominantly concerned with schools, it is worth briefly considering the nature of private education outside schools as well, for it is now possible to have private education almost from cradle to grave. At the pre-school level, out of a total of some 468,000 children aged 2–4 in full-time education in schools, 6 per cent were in the private sector. Also going private were 7 per cent of the 230,000 part-time pupils. However, this does not include the very large number of schools which cater for nursery children only, where private provision predominates, but about which the Department of Education and Science does not collect data.

In the same way there is no central record of the supplementary schooling that occurs in many cities, a form of private education which may very well not be seen as such by the participants involved. McLean (1985) suggests that participation in supplementary schooling by children of the major linguistic and ethnic minorities ranges from 10 to 75 per cent, and includes those of Japanese, Jewish, Polish, Greek Cypriot, Indian, and West Indian descent. Chevannes and Reeves (1987), on the other hand, argue that only a very small proportion of Afro-Caribbean children are involved in these private voluntary schools. Although induced by rather different concerns, parents of non-ethnic minority students have also wished to supplement the education received by their children in maintained schools. There has been a rapid growth in private tutors for GCSE-level work (Baker, 1987), and private tutorial colleges, or 'crammers', have blossomed for A-level students (Maitland, 1988).

At the post-school level it is possible for anyone to sell education and training, subject only to the usual restrictions on private business. There is no official control or monitoring of quality or efficiency and, while a number of independent accreditation agencies exist, such as the British Accreditation Council for Independent Further and Higher Education, non-membership does not necessarily reflect poor quality. As the Manpower Services Commission (1987) state, 'The size of this sector is uncertain; there is no complete register of institutions. They quote one study which identified 1,450 institutions, with the largest areas covered being health and beauty (24 per cent); business, secretarial, and professional (20 per cent); and languages and related activities (19 per cent). Private education and training within YTS and other MSC/Training Commission schemes have also expanded rapidly (Walford, 1987a). Finally, in 1983 the government authorized a royal charter to a private college in Buckingham which thus became the University of Buckingham, Britain's first and only private university.

The size of the private school sector

It is worth remembering that before 1870 all schools in Britain were private schools, for it was only in that year that the government of the day began to establish a network of state owned and maintained elementary schools. Glennerster and Wilson (1970) estimate that there were some 2.5 million pupils in private schools in the 1850s, but the quality of education offered to most of the pupils was very different from that obtainable in present-day private schools.

By the start of the Second World War over 90 per cent of the population from 5 to 14 were being educated in state maintained elementary schools, some of which were run by the Churches. Most of the remainder were educated in fee-paying private schools throughout. There was some small overlap, though, for about 10 per cent of the pupils in the maintained elementary schools moved out into grammar schools on scholarship places when aged 11. Most of these pupils went to maintained county grammar schools, but from 1926 some pupils also transferred into the private sector direct grant grammar schools.

The experience of the war years led to a tentative consensus about the need to build a 'land fit for heroes'. Free secondary education for all was part of the provision planned during the war years within the overall concept of the welfare state. The White Paper *Educational Reconstruction*, which was presented to Parliament in July 1943, proposed a radical reorganization of education. From the point of view of the private sector, the most important aspect was the way in which the bulk of the Church owned private secondary schools were to be included within a new maintained sector usually with either voluntary aided or voluntary controlled status. After the passing of the Act, the majority of both Roman Catholic and Church of England schools were largely funded by the state in order to provide a plannable educational system for all. By 1951 only 564,000 pupils remained in private and direct grant schools, representing about 9.2 per cent of the school population.

Table 1 gives an indication of how the proportion of pupils in private schools has varied since 1951. A full analysis is given by Halsey *et al.* (1984), but it is worth emphasizing some of the important trends. The general picture is one of continuous contraction of the private sector's share until the late 1970s, then a slight upturn in 1981 for most age groups, and a significant increase throughout the age range by 1987.

At the primary level, for most of the period, there was a decline in the absolute numbers in private schools, despite the fact that until the mid-1970s the size of the age group was on the increase. Halsey *et al.* (1984) argue that this decline was linked with the popularity of educationally progressive state maintained primary schools. These primary schools took the pupils who previously would largely have attended those schools 'not recognized as efficient' by the DES. It was this 'tail' of small and fairly cheap latter-day 'dame schools' which specialized in coaching for the 11 + that gradually disappeared, rather than the elite preparatory schools. If this interpretation is correct, then it would appear that parents became increasingly dissatisfied with state maintained primary schools as the 1970s and 1980s progressed. The proportion of 5–10-year-olds in private education went up by more than 10 per cent between 1981 and 1987.

Table 1 Full-time pupils, by age and type of school (%)

Year	Type of school	Age 5–10	11–15	16+	All
1951	Maintained	93.1	88.9	62.1	90.8
	Direct grant	0.4	2.4	9.3	1.4
	Private	6.5	8.7	28.7	7.8
	Total ('000)	3,614	2,404	131	6,149
1956	Maintained	94.0	89.5	67.2	91.7
	Direct grant	0.4	2.5	10.0	1.4
	Private	5.5	8.1	22.8	6.9
	Total ('000)	4,312	2,657	165	7,133
1961	Maintained	94.3	91.2	71.9	92.2
	Direct grant	0.5	2.2	9.1	1.5
	Private	5.2	6.5	19.0	6.2
	Total ('000)	3,907	3,140	253	7,300
1966	Maintained	95.1	91.2	77.7	92.7
	Direct grant	0.5	2.6	7.6	1.6
	Private	4.5	6.2	14.7	5.7
	Total ('000)	4,204	3,049	354	7,607
1971	Maintained	96.0	92.3	81.8	93.9
	Direct grant	0.4	2.4	6.9	1.5
	Private	3.6	5.2	11.2	4.6
	Total ('000)	4,804	3,300	418	8,522
1976	Maintained	96.2	93.3	86.2	94.4
	Direct grant	0.4	2.1	5.4	1.4
	Private	3.4	4.7	8.5	4.3
	Total ('000)	4,738	3,998	574	9,310
1981	Maintained	95.3	93.4	82.2	93.8
	Private	4.8	6.6	17.8	6.2
	Total ('000)	3,903	3,794	383	8,080
1987	Maintained	94.9	92.2	81.1	92.9
	Private	5.2	7.8	19.0	7.1
	Total ('000)	3,356	3,147	360	6,863

Notes. Based on Halsey *et al*. (1984), table 1.
Source. DES *Statistics of Education* and DES (1988). For 1951 and 1956 the figures for independent schools not recognized as efficient were estimated. Figures for 1981 and 1987 relate to England only, not England and Wales, as for the earlier years.

At the secondary level, if the direct grant schools are counted within the private sector, the absolute number of pupils remained relatively steady over a thirty-year period from 1951. The decline in the proportion is due to the two 'baby booms' of 1946 and 1961 and then the raising of the leaving age in 1973. The recent overall increase in the percentage of secondary pupils in private schools is the result of the schools actually increasing their intake at a time of falling school rolls nationally. A similar pattern is seen in the figures for those staying on after the school leaving age. Absolute numbers of 16+ pupils increased by over one-third in the thirty years from 1951, but the corresponding increase in the state sector was nearly 300 per cent. But, again, there has been a dramatic turnround in the trend in the last decade, such that the proportion of sixth-form pupils in private schools has now risen to nearly one-fifth again.

Table 2 Full-time primary and secondary school population in England, 1970–87 ('000)

Year	Total (all ages)	Private	% private
1970	7,998	521	6.5
1971	8,188	515	6.3
1972	8,378	516	6.2
1973	8,521	521	6.1
1974	8,864	528	6.0
1975	8,915	530	5.9
1976	8,960	523	5.8
1977	8,955	519	5.8
1978	8,861	510	5.8
1979	8,755	512	5.8
1980	8,593	517	6.0
1981	8,377	516	6.2
1982	8,147	510	6.3
1983	7,905	503	6.4
1984	7,717	500	6.5
1985	7,569	501	6.6
1986	7,441	504	6.8
1987	7,332	515	7.0

Source. DES (1988).

A more detailed time series for the whole of the English private sector is given in table 2. It can be seen that, while the total number of primary and secondary school pupils has steadily declined by about 20 per cent from 1976 onwards, since 1984 there has been a gradual increase in the actual numbers in the private sector. The long-term decrease in pupils was felt much more heavily in the maintained sector than in the private sector, such that the private schools have gradually increased their market share by about 20 per cent since 1978. Most of these pupils are in schools in membership of the major associations discussed earlier. Table 3 shows the figures for the schools in England only. It can be seen that nearly four-fifths of all pupils are to be found in these major associations, and that the big three – HMC, GSA/GBGSA and IAPS – account for 65 per cent of private pupils. Just over 25 per cent of pupils in these schools are boarders.

Table 3 Pupils in the major associations of schools, England only

Association	No. of schools	Boarding	Day	Total	% of all % of all private pupils
HMC	197	42,796	82,926	125,722	24.4
SHMIS	41	7,515	7,028	14,543	2.8
GBA	14	1,416	4,857	6,273	1.2
GSA/GBGSA	227	21,087	83,614	104,701	20.3
IAPS	513	25,547	80,917	106,464	20.7
ISAI	228	4,554	42,987	47,541	9.2
Totals		102,915	302,329	405,244	78.6

Source: ISIS (1988)

Summary

Discussion about private education and privatization of education frequently lacks detailed knowledge of the diversity of the schools in the private sector. This chapter describes the variety of different types of schools in Britain. It looks in particular at schools with headmasters in membership of the Headmasters' Conference and schools in membership of the Girls' Schools Association and the Incorporated Association of Preparatory Schools, but it also documents the wide range of schools which exist outside these major groups. The chapter also outlines the changes in the size of the sector that have occurred over time, and shows a gradual increase in the proportion of children privately educated since 1978.

Chapter two

Politics and private schools

In order to understand what is presently occurring in education, and the moves towards privatization of the system, it is necessary to have some knowledge of how the present educational system developed. This chapter gives an outline of English educational history, presented in such a way that the changing balance between private and public provision is evident. It attempts to show how decisions about the nature of provision and the form that provision should take have been the result of political decision-making processes.

For education is inherently political. There are choices to be made about what knowledge is to be taught, how it is to be taught, and to whom it is to be taught, and it is necessary to recognize that one of the great threads which runs through the history of education is the conflict between education as a liberating and egalitarian influence and education as a way of justifying elitism and privilege. In particular, there has been a strong tendency for England's educational system to be divided according to social class, with different educational experiences being provided for children from various social class backgrounds. As a result of political activity, the extent and nature of these divisions have varied over time – sometimes sharp and clear, sometimes less so – but differential provision according to social class has remained a major feature of English education.

Education before 1944

Before the nineteenth century the education of children was considered to be the private affair of parents. All schools were private schools. Those with sufficient means could employ private tutors for their children or send them to a variety of grammar or other fee-paying schools. Many of these grammar schools were the forebears of the present HMC private schools.

Schooling for the poor, if they had any schooling at all, was in dame schools and charity schools, and it is on this base that the maintained

19

sector was built. Over the centuries, and even at one particular time, the quality of schooling given in dame schools varied considerably. Perhaps in most cases they were little more than a child-minding service where younger women could leave their children under the care of an older one for a few pence a week. At their best, though, children might be taught reading and writing, and a few of the dame schools eventually developed into the preparatory schools for the major private schools (Leinster-Mackay, 1984). The charity school movement can be said to have started with the founding of the Society for Promoting Christian Knowledge (SPCK) in 1698 (Morrish, 1970), whose schools were intended to restore morals and religions to the poor children of what it perceived as an increasingly degenerate country. The schools were supported by the Churches, both through direct charitable donations and through the local clergy often teaching in the schools for no fee. As urbanization and industrialization progressed, the sometimes contradictory drives of philanthropy, religious conviction, and the practical need for a better educated and disciplined work force led to the gradual expansion of a network of schools for the poor.

The first formal involvement of the state in education was the Health and Morals of Apprentices Act of 1802, introduced by Sir Robert Peel, which forced employers to provide for the teaching of apprentices during the working day and for at least an hour on Sundays. This was later followed by two parliamentary committees in 1816 and 1818 which attempted to survey the extent and nature of elementary education available for the 'lower orders'. As expected, the reports chronicled 'grave deficiencies in general provision, accommodation and actual teaching' (Morrish, 1970), but the resulting first attempt to establish a national education system failed completely, as it became embroiled in a religious controversy over control. The Church of England wanted overall control of any new system; not surprisingly, the Roman Catholic and other Protestant Churches objected.

The next move to establish a national system was made in 1833. This failed as well, but it did lead to the first grant of £20,000 being made by government to aid 'private subscription for the erection of school houses'. The grant aid was paid to the two main religious providers of schooling at the time – the National Society for Promoting the Education of the Poor and the British and Foreign School Society. It is worth recognizing that, while this first grant is often regarded as the start of the maintained education system, it can equally well be seen as the start of government's financial and ideological support for the private and charitable sector of education. The estimated cost of providing a national service financed entirely by the state was long regarded as prohibitive (and still is, of course!), and it was not until 1870 that government even started to build and finance its own schools.

Grants to the private charity schools grew considerably after 1833, such that by 1856 an Education Department was established by the government to control this funding. Although they recognized the need to ensure that education was provided, the Victorian governments of the time were happy to leave this to the charitable organizations wherever possible, and would only help financially where other sources were insufficient. The establishment of an Education Department was soon accompanied by a series of Commissions into educational provision, each Commission – Clarendon, Taunton, and Newcastle – largely concentrating on provision for a particular social class.

The Newcastle Commission was charged to enquire into 'the present state of popular education in England', and was instructed to consider what measures, if any, were required for the extension of 'sound and cheap elementary instruction to all classes of the people'. In its report of 1861 the Commission found that some 95 per cent of children of the poorer classes attended school, even if only for four to six years, but it considered that the standard of teaching was low. It recommended that payment of government grant should be according to results, and that schools should be regularly inspected. This suggestion was incorporated in the now notorious Revised Code of 1863, which established six standards, said to correspond to the level of achievement expected from each of the six years of school life from age 7 onwards. Grant aid was not available for children aged over 12, and was paid to school managers, who were then to pay teachers according to how well children in each class achieved under examination. The similarities between this testing and that introduced by the 1988 Education Reform Act should not be overstated, but it is worth noting that this first attempt to introduce a national curriculum, like the 1988 version, was confined to the mass of the population, while children of the upper and middle classes attending non-government-supported private schools were not so constrained.

While the Newcastle Commission concerned itself mainly with the provision of elementary education for the poor, the two other Commissions investigated schooling for the more fortunate, who attended a variety of grammar, endowed, and other private schools. These schools often had long histories. It is estimated that by the later Middle Ages, for example, there were about 300 so-called grammar schools in England, some with up to 200 pupils. These were often the descendants of bishops' schools and were usually still closely linked with the Church. They had originally been founded to train boys to enter the Church or the law, and the curriculum had often been set by statute and had remained unchanged over the centuries. The number of grammar schools expanded during the sixteenth and seventeenth centuries, with numerous schools being established and endowed by rich merchants and businessmen. In addition, small local grammar schools began to expand and attract a national clientele such that, by the middle of the nineteenth century, Tom Brown's Universe (Honey, 1977), a system of private schools for the affluent, had been established. Most of these schools had a wider curriculum than the medieval schools, and began to challenge their supremacy. They included more modern subjects, such as English and science, and questions began to be asked about change within the Great Schools.

The Clarendon Commission was charged to enquire into the management and curriculum of the 'Great Schools' – which were taken to be Eton, Winchester, Westminster, St Paul's, Merchant Taylors', Harrow, Rugby, Charterhouse, and Shrewsbury. Within the group, Rugby and Shrewsbury had already moved towards a broader curriculum, as had Marlborough, Cheltenham, and Wellington, which were also examined by Clarendon as examples of recently founded schools. The Public Schools Act which eventually followed in 1868 had far less effect than the report intended. It reformed the governing bodies and organization of most of these schools, but allowed them to maintain their position as 'the chief nurseries of our statesmen'.

In 1864 the third Commission, that under Lord Taunton, investigated the secondary schools which had not been considered by the Clarendon Commission. These included some 780 grammar schools, many other private and proprietary schools, and the secondary schools for girls. It established that there were more than 1,000 individually owned private profit-making schools, as well as many proprietary schools owned by companies (Robinson, 1971). The Endowed Schools Bill followed in 1869, Part II of which proposed a substantial amount of government intervention into the activities and autonomy of the endowed schools. Headmasters of the leading endowed schools rose to the threat, and two meetings took place between some of those headmasters of endowed schools which ranked themselves just below the Great Schools. Edward Thring, headmaster of Uppingham, proposed a regular meeting of such Heads, and the Headmasters' Conference was born (Leinster-Mackay, 1987). In part owing to pressure from these headmasters, Part II of the Act, which envisaged setting up a national council to oversee the endowed schools, was never put into effect. By contrast, the Endowed School Commissioners implemented the major part of the Act with considerable zeal. They reorganized school endowments in such a way that three grades of school for the middle classes were established, each grade charging a set fee and each having a specific purpose. Endowments originally intended to provide free education for all children in a locality were abolished, and the income was used instead to reduce fees for the middle classes and provide some free places in the form of competitive scholarships. In practice, as Musgrave (1968: 39) recounts, 'By 1873 over 300 schemes had been drawn up . . . . There was a tendency for these schemes . . . to direct monies from the provision of working-class education to the establishment of new secondary schools for the middle-class.' Foundations which had once served poor and working-class children were transformed into thoroughly middle-class institutions.

The long-term result of the three Commissions was to ensure that the divide between the private and state sectors largely coincided with class divisions. The 1870 Forster Act closely followed the three Commissions and successfully constructed a national elementary education system. It avoided the problem of Church of England control by providing for the continued existence of the voluntary Church schools alongside state maintained board schools. The board schools were to be established only in those areas where there were gaps in the Church provision. This compromise was the start of the dual system which still exists, whereby the county schools are under the control of local education authorities and Church schools remain the province of the various Church denominations. In England and Wales the state maintained sector thus contains within it schools owned and controlled by the Roman Catholic Church and the Church of England, while in many other countries such denominationally based schools were excluded from the developing state systems and thus have remained as the major part of the private sector (Walford, 1989).

This inclusion of most of the Church schools into the state system meant that class divisions became clearer in education. By the end of the century working-class education had become almost entirely under state control either directly or indirectly, while that for the upper class had become synonymous with the reformed Clarendon schools, those included in the Headmasters' Conference, and the growing number of private schools for girls. These schools were fed by the growing number of preparatory schools, which prepared children for entry to the major schools in isolation from children of other social classes. Education for the middle classes was more mixed, but differed from that of the working class in that it was much more likely that middle-class children would continue education beyond compulsory school leaving age.

The state's increased involvement in education led to the 1902 Education Act, which established the local education authorities, which were required to maintain all public elementary schools, whether council or voluntary. Secondary education was available only to some – either those with money to pay substantial fees, or to those passing a special scholarship examination.

The Labour Party grew rapidly during the early part of the twentieth century, and it is only at this point that it becomes reasonable to start to consider the development of the educational policies of modern-day political parties. The Labour party's historical roots in the labour and union movements meant that its fundamental educational concern has been to expand educational provision for all children. Coupled with this has been a desire to reduce class divisions, which has irregularly emerged as an attack on private education when it was seen as perpetuating these divisions and fostering privilege. During the 1920s and 1930s the Labour Party's main educational concerns were with attempting to bring secondary education to all children, and it made several attempts to do so. The lack of success was due to the strong opposition from Conservative and National governments' fear of great expenditure at a time of severe economic depression. By the 1930s, however, most pupils were in elementary education until 14, with a few moving at 11, through scholarship examination, into grammar schools or direct grant schools. This scholarship ladder of personal social mobility was not simply for the benefit of the individual children selected. It allowed the ruling and middle classes to absorb some of the most intelligent and able children of the working class, and thus maintain and justify their position.

The direct grant schools to which some working-class children gained entry through scholarships were an interesting group of schools which have been the subject of considerable political controversy. They were not created to be a separate and distinct group at all, but were to have functions similar to those of other secondary schools. They came about in 1926. Prior to that date, secondary schools controlled by voluntary bodies could receive grants from central government, from local government, or from both. Circular 1381 in 1926 simplified this situation by ensuring that schools could receive grants from central or local government, but not from both. The direct grant schools were simply those private secondary schools which after that date received their grant direct from central government. They acted as grammar schools to which children could transfer at 11 on scholarship awards or on payment of fees. Their distribution was uneven and concentrated in the north of England and Lancashire. In other regions there were more grammar schools which received their grant from the local education authority or which were fully controlled and maintained by the LEAs.

The 1944 Education Act

The Second World War marked a turning point in education policy, just as it did for so many other welfare services. It was not simply that the evacuation of poor children from London forced the affluent to recognize the extent of their own educational advantage, or that the 'one nation' that had been created through the war effort automatically led to a more egalitarian future. It was that the promise of a better future for those actually fighting and for their children was a central part of the war effort itself. Planning for a new educational system, which was seen as a vital part of Beveridge's proposed welfare state, started only a few years into the war. Debate continued as the war deepened, and such planning played a vital part in raising the morale of the forces by giving them 'something to fight for'. The White Paper *Educational Reconstruction* was presented to Parliament in July 1943 – the same month that Allied forces made their re-entry into Europe from Africa through Sicily. At times like these a programme of rapid widening of educational opportunity for the mass of the population mattered more than any concern about the maintenance of elitism. The White Paper hardly mentioned private schools, merely stating that it was the government's intention 'to devise ways and means by which these schools can be more closely associated with the national system'. Instead, it promised an end to all fee payment in the maintained sector and introduced secondary schooling for all as a distinct stage of education from 11 to 15, and later to 16. More fundamentally with regard to the state/private division, it set out the results of detailed negotiations with the Churches on ways in which the Church primary and secondary schools would become fully integrated with the maintained sector through voluntary controlled or voluntary aided status.

This planned expansion of the state sector was seen as something of a threat by many of the private secondary schools not controlled by the Churches. The last few years before the war had not been kind to these schools, as there had been a falling birth rate coupled with prospective parents being hit by the economic depression of the 1930s. Many of the schools were not in a particularly good shape to face a direct challenge. Thus it was partly in recognition of the more egalitarian feelings of the time, and partly in trying to ensure their continued existence, that in 1942 the HMC persuaded R.A. Butler to establish the Flemming Committee 'to consider means whereby the association between the Public Schools . . . and the general educational system of the country could be developed and extended'. The report of the committee in 1944 recommended that the schools should be open to all who could benefit from them, irrespective of income. This was seen not only as a benefit to the pupils involved but also to the schools in overcoming the 'serious weakness' that they 'too often concerned themselves with children coming from only a limited section of society' (quoted in Rae, 1981: 26). The report suggested two schemes. The first was designed mainly for the direct grant schools, while the second offered individual awards to pupils from the maintained sector to become boarders in HMC or GBA schools. These means-tested places would be administered and paid for by the Ministry of Education, while the LEAs could have their own bursary schemes if they wished. It was intended that a minimum of 25 per cent of the intake of each school should be in the scheme. The schools, although wary about the 25 per cent minimum, were generally keen to experiment within the terms of the proposals.

Sir Robert Birley who was a member of the Flemming Committee, suggests (Rae, 1981: 27) that there was a broad consensus from both Labour and Conservative sides for some sort of scheme which would broaden access to the major private schools. Scholarships and special places for able children were part of the accepted ideology, which had equality of educational opportunity as its goal. Birley suggests that had the Conservatives won the 1945 election a scheme on the Flemming lines would have been introduced. In practice, Labour won and the scheme floundered, not because of any outright opposition from Labour, but because the new Labour MPs had more experience of local rather than national politics and thus wanted such a scheme to be under the control of local government. While a few bursaries were given, the LEAs were generally not interested, as they put the building of a new tripartite secondary system as their first priority.

While those private schools not receiving government grant remained unchanged by the 1944 Education Act the direct grant schools did not. The 231 schools that were at that time receiving direct grant were given the choice of continuing the direct grant on new terms, joining the maintained sector, or reverting to private status without grant. The new terms under which the schools were to operate were intended to bring them into a closer relationship with the maintained sector, and were a modification of the Flemming Report (1944) proposals. The schools were required to have at least 25 per cent of pupils on free places, and filled by pupils who had been educated for at least two years in a maintained or grant-aided primary school. These places were usually paid for by the local education authorities, but some were financed through foundation income, or through increased fees for the remaining fee-paying pupils. In addition to this 25 per cent of free places, local education authorities had the right, if they wished, to pay for further free places up to 50 per cent of the total. If the governors agreed, the authorities could go beyond this figure, and in 1969, for example, more than half the schools had more than half their places as free places. In total, over 60 per cent of the places in direct grant schools were free at this time (Public Schools Commission, 1970a) and were usually awarded on the basis of competitive examination at age 10. The remaining places were available to fee-payers, but even here the fee payable was calculated on the basis of an income-related means test, and the Department of Education and Science paid the difference between the amount paid by parents and the school's fees.

In 1969 there were 178 direct grant schools, and they educated about 3 per cent of the secondary school population, including about 10 per cent of the sixth-form pupils. There was considerable diversity of schools in terms of size, and the extent of boarding provision, but the key feature about the schools was that, in 1968, all but one were academically selective. In practice, many of the schools were treated by local authorities, and by pupils and parents, as part of the local authority selective education system. They served the function of the local grammar school, especially for Roman Catholics. Fee-payers were in the minority, with only 28 per cent paying full fees, and a further 9 per cent paying partial fees, overall.

It was this close association with the maintained sector that eventually led to the direct grant being phased out in 1975 by the Labour government. Rather than being an attack on the direct grant schools as such, the decision was based on the desire to introduce a fully comprehensive state system, and it was their selectivity within the extended state system which was crucial.

The 1944 Education Act had made secondary education a distinct stage for all children. In the years immediately following the war, secondary schools were provided to accommodate all children 'according to age, ability, and aptitude', which, at that time, was generally interpreted in terms of the ideas put forward in the Norwood and Spens Reports. These reports embodied ideas about meritocracy, and beliefs from psychology about the necessity for separate provision for three types of pupil. Equality of opportunity demanded that every individual should be given the same opportunity of educational and occupational success, but only in that they should be treated alike until relevant grounds were established for treating them differently. These relevant criteria were assumed, by practically everyone, to be ability and aptitude rather than class, wealth, or income, and it was also assumed that judgements about relative ability should be delayed until as late as possible in a child's life. Equality of opportunity was seen as a desirable goal, both for reasons of fairness for individuals and in terms of society's need to ensure that highly skilled jobs were occupied by the most able. It was widely accepted that selection of children according to ability was in the best interests of both the child and society. Separate provision in grammar, technical, or modern schools was proposed, to enable children to develop their talents and to fit them for their future place in the occupational structure.

Such a massive reconstruction of the educational system following a devastating war meant that any attempt to deal with integration of the private schools was pushed into the background. It is not clear that Clement Attlee's Labour government of 1945–51 even had the political will to try to deal with them, for Attlee and many of those in the government had themselves been educated in such schools and still saw them as models to be emulated by the grammar schools in a state system. What is certain is that such changes were not a priority.

Throughout the history of the Labour Party there has been a curious lack of cohesion over the question of what to do about private education. Many trade unionists and members of the party have fiercely attacked the schools for their elitism and snobbery and for the role which they see the schools as having in perpetuating privilege and inequality. They are seen as a symbol of the nature and permanence of class divisions. However, in their election manifestoes, and in government, Labour have often been more circumspect in their criticism, and more aware of the dilemmas about abolishing private schools in a democratic society. Labour left office in 1951 with no clear plans for the further integration or abolition of the private schools. They reformulated their views during their long period in opposition.

Comprehensive education

The tripartite system was not to last long. In most areas the technical schools hardly got off the ground, so that selection at 11+ became a contest where those who 'passed' went to grammar schools, while the majority who 'failed' ended up in the secondary moderns. Moreover, during the 1950s evidence was gradually gained showing that there was considerable class bias between the two or three types of school in the tripartite system. It seemed that the new system was reinforcing class divisions rather than offering wider opportunities to all. Arguments centred on the inability of the 11+ examination to discriminate adequately between children according to their differing academic potential, and on the examinations having to be taken at too early an age, while children were still developing at different rates. It was also shown that children could be coached into obtaining high scores in their examinations, and that the reliability of the tests was low (Ford, 1969).

A further important factor was that there was an increasing demand for a 'grammar-school-type' education. This was probably due to rising expectations on the part of parents, but also to the effects of the post-war 'bulge' in population, where expansion of the system had resulted in only a very few new grammar school places. Middle-class parents were finding that their children were not being admitted to the grammar schools which they themselves had attended, but instead were attending secondary modern schools which were often funded at a lower level, had poorer paid and less qualified teachers, and were able to enter children for only a limited range of examinations. Whilst this partisan demand could have been dealt with through an expansion of grammar schools, self-interest (even on behalf of sons and daughters) was largely transmuted publicly into a plea for greater equality of educational provision, which was often in terms of comprehensive schools.

While the popular demands for comprehensive education were in terms of equality of opportunity, there were also a rather smaller number of educationalists and intellectuals on the left pressing for greater equality. Comprehensive schools were seen by this group as a way of reducing class differences in society. They argued that putting all children into the same sort of school, where they would have equal access to high-quality teachers and to equal physical facilities, would bring greater equality within the schools and lead to greater equality outside in the world of work. It was hoped that mixing children from different class backgrounds in school would bring about a lowering of social class barriers and lead to a reduction in class antagonism and class differences.

As the 1950s progressed demands for comprehensive education increased, and the Labour Party became firmly committed to the abolition of selection and to the comprehensive ideal in 1955. At the same time there were pressures to deal with what was seen by some to be a far greater cause for concern – the private schools. Anthony Crosland, for example, saw the public schools as 'the strongest remaining bastion of class privilege' and stated that he had 'never been able to understand why socialists had been so obsessed with the question of the grammar schools, and so indifferent to the much more glaring injustice of the independent schools' (1956: 260). At the official level, the Labour Party was less clear about what to do. Rae (1981: 35) quotes the Labour Party's *Notes for Speakers* of 1958, which talked of the 'many different viewpoints about the public schools within the Labour Movement', and outlined some of the problems of possible abolition, of giving free places, and of leaving them unaltered. It proposed a vague plan whereby they might be integrated into the national scheme, but stressed that this was only a very long-term aim.

By the 1964 election the Labour Party had bowed to pressure from within and made both comprehensive education and an investigation of the private schools manifesto issues. On election, the Wilson government, with Crosland as Secretary of State for Education and Science, issued Circular 10/65 requesting all local education authorities to submit plans for reorganization on a comprehensive basis and also set up the Public Schools Commission. The commissioners were instructed in their terms of reference to seek ways of integrating the private schools into the state maintained system. The aim was not to abolish them, but to maintain and develop what was seen to be best in them within a wider comprehensive system. After some initial problems in finding a chairman for the Commission, John Newsom was appointed. The members included John Dancy, High Master of Marborough, who had already written of ways in which the schools might become better associated with the maintained sector (Dancy, 1963). The final report was not unanimous, and contained several minority views appended. The committee had studied the boarding schools in separation from the direct grant schools, and the majority view of the first was that they should be used to take up unmet 'boarding need' within the wider community (Public Schools Commission, 1968). This idea was one which had been floated within the Labour Party and elsewhere several years before, and the Department of Education and Science had already sponsored a research project to look at boarding education. This early work by Royston Lambert (1966) was incorporated within the first report and added weight to the suggestion that there were at least some 30,000 children with boarding need who could be accommodated within the proposed integrated boarding schools, in addition to the 20,000 places in boarding schools which were already being supported by the state. Ten categories of boarding need were identified, and if all these children had their needs met they would occupy about half the boarding places. No longer would the schools be socially exclusive!

The report was ignored by the Labour government when it was presented in April 1968. Few believed that unmet 'boarding need' was actually as great as suggested, or that boarding need and boarding demand would coincide in the convenient way that the report assumed. Nor was it accepted that 'changing half the bodies in the beds' would actually deal with the perceived elitism of the schools, and those on the left of the party still wished to abolish the schools outright rather than attempt any integration. Finally, the cost of the Commission's scheme would have been enormous. The establishment of the Commission had allowed Harold Wilson to claim that he was actually doing something about the private schools, but he clearly felt under no obligation to follow its recommendations when it eventually reported.

The second report of the Public Schools Commission was to have a more lasting long-term effect. The Commission's terms of reference had been extended in 1967 such that they were also instructed to look at the direct grant schools – to review the principle of central government grant and to advise on the best ways in which the schools might participate in the movement towards comprehensive reorganization. As described earlier, as the direct grant schools were very closely associated with the maintained sector, and all but one were academically selective, they were a clear anachronism in an increasingly comprehensive system. It made little sense to continue to fund the direct grant schools while abolishing selection within the maintained sector, and the Commission duly recommended that the grant should cease. It did not, however, recommend the abolition of the schools, but suggested that the direct grant grammar schools and the private day schools should be given the option of entering the maintained sector as fully maintained comprehensive schools. If they did not wish to do this, the Commission believed, they would be allowed to continue as private schools, being funded by full fees paid by parents.

The second report was presented in January 1970. Again there was no action from the government, but this time it was probably because a general election was called in June. Labour lost, and the new

Conservative government maintained its strong support for this 'ladder of opportunity' for able students.

The Labour Party's attacks on the private sector have always been stronger when it has been in opposition than when in power. By 1973 the Labour party had firmly committed itself to abolition of all direct grant and private schools. The party and the education spokesman, Roy Hattersley, put forward a step-by-step plan for the gradual reduction of all government subsidy to the schools, including the removal of charitable status, and their eventual abolition by prohibiting the charging of fees for full-time schooling. The direct grant would be quickly phased out. Hattersley's arguments centred on three factors – that the schools were socially divisive, that they diverted energy and enthusiasm away from the maintained sector, and that they consumed a disproportionate share of scarce resources (Rae, 1981: 51). The Conservative government had only a moderate majority, so the threats were taken very seriously by the private schools and those who wished them to continue.

The private and direct grant schools had gradually responded to the Labour Party's growing hostility to them over the 1960s. In 1966 the Direct Grant Joint Committee had been formed, which became a very effective pressure group on their behalf. In particular, it had put forward an early assisted places scheme which attempted to extend the scope of the direct grant and overcome its greatest weakness – that of financing pupils without respect to parental income (Whitty *et al.*, 1989). The HMC had also established a public relations unit, and in 1972 the independent schools in the major associations recognized that some aggressive marketing would help their case, and established the Independent Schools Information Service. The Independent Schools Joint Council was formed in 1974 to provide a co-ordinating agency and pressure group for the various bodies within the private sector.

The Labour Party's general election manifesto for the February 1974 election concerned itself only with the first steps towards removing what it saw as privilege within education – the abolition of tax reforms and charitable status. Labour won (twice) in 1974, and swiftly announced that the direct grant would be phased out from 1975 and that schools could choose either to enter the maintained sector or remain as private schools without grant. By 1978 some 60 out of 178 schools, mainly Roman Catholic, had chosen to enter the maintained sector; the rest opted for full independent status, no doubt hoping that a future government might restore some sort of grant in due course. As individual pupils were supported, and fees were to be continued for pupils already in the schools, the phasing out of the grant was fairly slow, and some schools were still receiving the remnants of direct grant as late as 1984.

The direct effect of Labour's move was to increase the number of private schools, but this was seen as a necessary first step, before market forces ensured the closure of some of them and government action eventually made all fee-paying schools illegal. The government wished to help ensure that these market forces were fully felt by removing government subsidy to all private schools as well. The number of pupils in private schools paid by LEAs was reduced in 1976 by forcing the authorities to seek approval from the Secretary of State for each place. In practice, while most of the applications were approved, fewer places were offered. A further aspect was the removal of charitable status. Here the government did not redeem its election promise, and by 1977 claimed that a special small group of lawyers had failed to achieve a satisfactory way of redefining charitable activities such that Save the Children Fund and Oxfam did not lose government exemptions as well as the private schools. Legal definitions are difficult, of course, but it cannot be beyond the ability of government to devise a satisfactory law if the political will is really there. That Labour failed to move on this point indicates a weakening of resolve once more when in office. By October 1976 James Callaghan had given his Ruskin College speech, launched the 'Great Debate', and largely forgotten the private schools issue once more.

Labour entered the 1979 election still with the promise to end charitable status for private schools, but we did not get the chance to find out whether this would actually have been done.

Present political positions

In 1980 the Labour Party published a sizeable booklet entitled *Private Schools*. In it was presented a detailed case against private education, in terms of purchase of educational, social, and occupational privilege, damage to the maintained sector, social isolation of pupils in such schools, and cost in subsidy to the Exchequer. The booklet outlined the various ways in which it was proposed that any future Labour government would act to gradually abolish private education. In a phased process, very similar to that suggested by Roy Hattersley some years earlier, it was proposed to withdraw all public support for the schools, revoke their charitable status, and eventually prohibit charging of fees for schooling. The Labour Party and the TUC published a policy document on private schools in July 1981 which was based upon the previous discussion document. It was presented and endorsed by Neil Kinnock, as Shadow Education Secretary, and still forms the basis of Labour's policy for the sector.

In its 1983 election manifesto, for example, Labour stated:

Private schools are a major obstacle to a free and fair education system, able to serve the needs of the whole community. We will abolish the Assisted Places Scheme and local authority place buying; and we will phase out, as quickly as possible, boarding allowances paid to government personnel for their children to attend private schools whilst ensuring secure accommodation for children needing residential education.

We shall also withdraw charitable status from private schools and all their other public subsidies and tax privileges. We will also charge VAT on the fees paid to such schools; phase out fee charging; and integrate private schools within the local authority sector where necessary. Special schools for handicapped pupils will retain all current support and tax advantages.

[Labour Party, 1983: 21]

By the 1987 election manifesto, however, Labour was being much more careful in its attack on the schools. The manifesto as a whole was much thinner, and the section on private schools had been reduced to:

At the same time as we improve the quality of publicly provided education, we shall end the 11 plus everywhere and stop the diverting of precious resources that occurs through the Assisted Places Scheme and the public subsidies to private schools.

[Labour Party, 1987: 9]

In various reported interviews, however, both Neil Kinnock, as leader of the party, and Roy Hattersley, as deputy leader, were saying that they hoped eventually to abolish fee-paying for schooling (*ISIS News*, 1987).

In 1983 the newly formed Alliance did not mention private schools in its manifesto, but ISIS obtained the following statement from them which it then published:

We would not abolish the independent schools. The free society to which we are committed could not take away the right of parents to pay for the education they choose for their children. But we would not subsidise those who attend independent schools.

We seek ways in which the private and state sectors of education can co-operate together for the benefit of all. To this end we will:

• Reinstate the inspection, recognition and registration of independent schools – which will bring them into the same public scrutiny as the state schools. This is something many public schools have asked for and would welcome.

• We do not agree with schemes which simply cream off the most able children from the state sector. We would end new places under the Assisted Places Scheme and would not support any extension of a 'Voucher' system to state education.

• Review admission procedures to universities, especially Oxford and Cambridge, to make sure prospective students from state schools are not disadvantaged.

● We believe the benefits of charitable status should be confined to charitable activities, and we recommend a review of the charitable status of private schools as part of a major review of charity law.

[*ISIS Newsletter*, 1983]

By 1987 the Alliance were prepared to give education a major place in their manifesto and stated:

We recognise and would uphold the right of those who wish to pay for independent education in the private sector. We would phase out the Assisted Places Scheme without affecting pupils already in the scheme, so that money which has been diverted from the state system can once again be used to raise the standards in state schools. We believe that charitable tax reliefs in private education should only go to genuinely philanthropic activities, and would review the workings of charity law with that object in view. We will encourage greater co-operation between state and independent schools.

[SDP/Liberal Alliance, 1987: 15]

Education was given such prominence that a special ten-point plan for 'Investing in quality' was also produced for the manifesto, with at least the first five points appearing to apply to private schools:

● We will encourage all schools, both maintained and independent, to publish indicators showing progress in academic results related to intake and social factors such as community involvement, truancy, and delinquency.
● We will ask each school to set targets for improvement – in the case of maintained schools, in consultation with their local education authorities.
● We will institute 'special inspections' of all schools which regularly fall below a certain level in terms of progress achieved.
● We will institute an annual 'Queen's Award' for schools, to be judged by an independent panel of experts, for outstanding progress, teaching and curriculum innovation and success.
● We will establish 'teacher fellowships' as one year awards to outstanding teachers.

[SDP/Liberal Alliance, 1987: 14]

While Labour presented outright opposition, and the Alliance showed ambivalence, by 1983 the Conservative Party had become the 'natural' party to support the private schools. As the Labour party's pro-comprehensive stance had clarified during the 1960s, the private schools began to look for political supporters. At that time most, but not all, of these were to be found in the Conservative ranks. The direct grant schools, in particular, had long recognized the weakness of their position, and in the early 1970s had tried to persuade the Conservative government of the day to adopt a means-tested assisted places scheme instead of the direct grant, as this would have made them easier to defend from attack. At that point the Conservatives were not interested in making any changes, but, once the Labour government had begun to phase out the direct grant in 1975, it was much easier for the representatives of the private schools to negotiate with the Conservative Party to develop a form of assistance which suited them. There developed a close collaboration between representatives of the Conservative Party and those of the schools (Salter and Tapper, 1985), and they were able to negotiate a means-tested Assisted Places Scheme which was included in the party's 1979 election manifesto.

As the 1980s have progressed, the Conservative government has made more clear its support for all forms of private provision and service over those of the state. As will be discussed in detail in chapter four, privatization has been a key element of government policy in a variety of fields, and not least in education. The private schools have found themselves the recipients of considerable ideological and financial support. In 1983 the Conservative Party manifesto stated:

> Giving parents more power is one of the most effective ways of raising educational standards. We shall continue to seek ways of widening parental choice and influence over their children's schooling.
> We shall defend church schools and independent schools alike against our opponents' attacks. And we shall defend the right of parents to spend their own money on educating their children.
> [Conservative party, 1983]

The Conservatives chose to make education one of the major issues of their 1987 general election campaign, and to make the privatization of education the key to most of their policies in the area. They promised an Education Reform Act which would radically change the face of British education. The four major reforms promised were the establishment of a national curriculum, financial delegation of budgets to schools, an increase in parental choice, and provision to allow state schools to opt out of LEA control.

The resulting Education Reform Act of 1988 is the subject of chapter five, but it is worth quoting the manifesto's specific references to existing private schools:

> We will therefore support the co-existence of a variety of schools – comprehensive, grammar, secondary modern, voluntary controlled and aided, independent, sixth form and tertiary colleges . . . all of which will give parents a greater choice and lead to higher standards.

35

We will expand the Assisted Places Scheme to 35,000. This highly successful scheme has enabled 25,000 talented children from less-well-off backgrounds to gain places at the 230 independent schools currently in the scheme.

We will continue to defend the right to independent education as part of a free society. It is under threat from all the other parties.

[Conservative Party, 1987]

By 1987 the political parties had developed their own distinctive policies on private education, and there is good reason to believe that the Conservative view was one which helped them win. Some of the most reliable evidence of British attitudes towards a diversity of social issues is to be found in the series of surveys being conducted by Social and Community Planning Research. As has become usual, the 1986 British Social Attitudes Survey (Jowell *et al.*, 1987) contained questions on attitudes towards private schools. Jowel *et al.* interviewed 3,100 randomly selected people who formed a representative sample of those aged over 18. The large majority (64 per cent) wanted there to be about the same number of private schools as now, and 13 per cent wanted more such schools. Only 9 per cent wanted fewer schools, and a further 10 per cent wanted no private schools at all (3 per cent 'don't know' and 'other'). It would seem that only 19 per cent were in support of Labour's plans for abolition, while a massive 77 per cent gave some degree of support to the schools.

What is more remarkable is the growth in public support for private schools compared to the results of the previous year's British Social Attitudes survey (Jowell *et al.*, 1986). In 1985 a similar, although smaller, survey had found that 9 per cent had wanted more private schools, and 59 per cent about the same as now – a total of 68 per cent showing some degree of support, while 13 per cent wanted fewer private schools and 16 per cent no private schools at all. Thus in 1985 some 29 per cent were generally in favour of Labour's policy, while in 1986 the figure had dropped to just 19 per cent. The Conservative Party's outright support of private schools thus certainly did it little harm.

Just as interestingly, there appear to be a considerable number of Labour voters who support private schooling. Unfortunately the 1986 figures have not yet been published in a fully analysed form, but the 1985 survey found that 52 per cent of Labour supporters supported more private schools or wanted about the same as now. Only 11 per cent of Conservative voters wanted fewer or no private schools. There were also some 62 per cent of manual workers who supported private schools, and 65 per cent of those who had left full-time education aged 16 or under similarly supported private education. Only 25 per cent of Labour voters wanted there to be no private schools at all.

With such an overwhelming proportion of the population believing that other people had the right to have their children privately educated if they wished, it was not surprising that the Labour Party did not include an explicit promise to abolish private schools in its manifesto. Its known firm opposition, however, undoubtedly lost it votes and contributed to its third successive general election defeat.

Summary

This chapter has outlined the way in which educational provision in England and Wales developed. Before 1870 all schools were privately owned and controlled, and provision was largely dependent upon parents' ability and willingness to pay. A range of grades of school was available for children from different social class backgrounds, such there was little social mixing in schools and the education received was designed for future class-related occupations and 'stations in life'. After the 1870 Education Act the state began to build and maintain its own elementary schools in geographical areas where there were insufficient private charity schools for working-class children. The state's involvement in education grew, and scholarships were provided so that some working-class children were able to attend private and grammar schools.

The 1944 Education Act brought free secondary education for all. At first, differential provision continued through a tripartite system of maintained secondary education, in addition to a continuing private secondary sector. The selection of children for separate schooling, according to ability and aptitude, became a major political issue during the 1960s which then extended to include the debate over the remaining private sector. By the 1970s the major political parties had firm and opposed ideas about the benefits of retaining some private schools. The Labour Party wanted to cut all government support for the schools and eventually abolish the right for schools to charge fees, while the Conservative Party actively supported the private sector and championed freedom of choice and the right of parents to purchase education for their children if they wished.

Recent social surveys indicate that the Conservative party's support for private education is much more in line with positive public attitudes to private schools than is the oppositional stance of the Labour Party.

Chapter three

Can you buy privilege?

Attendance at a private school means something far more than an education. In Britain it is the basic requirement for membership of the hierarchy which still dominates so many positions of power and influence. Private school fees therefore buy more than examination success. They are the admission charge for a ruling elite whose wealth gives them the power and whose power gives them wealth. And the main means of transferring economic status, social position and influence from generation to generation is through a private education system which ensures that merit can be bought. This is one of the main reasons why the Labour Party finds the presence of the private schools in the education system so objectionable.

[Labour Party, 1980: 10]

The above quotation, from the Labour Party's most thorough policy document on private schools, indicates that the belief that social and occupational privilege can be purchased through private schools is one of the main objections that Labour sees to the continuance of private education. The statement takes it for granted that examination success can be purchased, and argues that it is also possible to buy and maintain a position in the elite through attendance at such schools.

At first sight there would appear to be good evidence to support this view. For example, although in 1988 only just above 7 per cent of the school population were in private schools, these schools provided about 25 per cent of undergraduates in British universities. For Oxford and Cambridge Universities the figure was just under a half. Pupils from private schools obtained about 25 per cent of all A-level passes, and 50 per cent of all A grades at A level. In 1984 at least 83 per cent of High Court judges and appeal judges, 69 per cent of ambassadors, 50 per cent of high-ranking civil servants, and 89 per cent of law lords had been to private schools (Reid, 1986). In 1981, 92 per cent of directors of major life insurance companies, 70 per cent of directors of clearing banks, 83 per cent of chairmen of clearing banks, and 88 per cent of chairmen of merchant banks (Sampson, 1982) had also spent their early years in these schools. Just under half the Members of Parliament in 1987 had been privately educated. In Scotland, where only about 4 per cent are in private schools, 41 per cent of a wide-ranging sample of 'people of influence' in 1986 had a private school background (Walford, 1987b).

These figures are certainly impressive, and they are just an indication of the long-standing relationship that exists between some elite private schools and positions of power and influence. The major private schools have traditionally had very close links with Oxford and Cambridge and, either through them or directly, with high-status professions. We saw in chapter two that the history of the private schools has been associated with the desire of wealthy parents to ensure that their own positions of privilege and prestige could be passed on to their children. But to find a relationship between attendance at a certain school and educational, social, and occupational success does not necessarily mean that that such attendance actually had any effect at all. Those children might have done just as well if they had attended state maintained schools instead. Further, even if we could show that the schools actually had an effect in the past, it does not mean that they still have an effect now or will continue do so in the future. Many of those at present in high positions of power and influence were in school before the 1944 Education Act introduced free secondary education for all. The educational system which they passed through was very different from that of today.

Whether or not privilege can be bought at private schools is thus a rather complicated question, and one where there are rather fewer applicable data to help us than is desirable. In particular, there is practically no sociological work on female elites or on the relationship between elite female status and attendance at a private school. Even if there were some data, they would be a very bad predictor of future relationships, simply because so many HMC schools now accept girls and women's position in society has changed so dramatically in the last few decades. A further difficulty is that most of the limited amount of research work available concentrates on the major schools only, in particular those in the HMC. It is usually assumed, but certainly not proven, that the less prestigious schools have no part to play in elite status. We saw in chapter one that there is an amazing variety of schools within the private sector, so that even if we find that some schools offer advantage, this is far from showing that all private schools do so. This chapter will investigate the available evidence to try to assess the extent to which economic and social inequality in society is related to attendance at such schools.

Which parents choose private schools?

Before investigating the question of whether or not privilege can be bought, it is useful to consider what sort of parents decide to use the private sector, and why they do so. The data available are very limited, and restricted to the major schools. A very different picture might emerge for parents using the cheaper or more unusual schools – we simply do not know.

The most detailed study of private school parents to date is that conducted by Irene Fox (1984, 1985). She interviewed the parents of 190 boys in traditional public (as opposed to ex-direct grant) schools. Just over half the boys were boarders. The parents were selected at random from a stratified sample of twenty of these schools, and intensive interviews were conducted in 1979–80. By working through the HMC and individual headmasters, Fox was able to get a remarkably high response rate of 88 per cent. Six per cent of the sample were non-contactable and only 6 per cent refused to be interviewed. In the present context there are obvious limitations to the data, in that they were obtained only from the parents of boys in the traditional part of the HMC sector, but the very high response rate does give considerable confidence in their generalizability within this group of parents.

The most surprising finding was that about half the total number of parents interviewed had been educated in the maintained sector (usually in grammar schools), and three-quarters of them had used the maintained sector for the whole or part of the education of some or all of their children. A quarter of the parents had at one time had at least one child in the maintained secondary school which would have been the alternative to the private school actually used. The majority of the parents thus had some direct knowledge of the maintained sector. Only 44 per cent of the fathers in the sample had themselves been privately educated, and only about one-tenth of the boys came from homes where private education was simply part of the general culture of the family and its friends and relations. Further, she found that the parents of boarders were remarkably similar to those of day boys, and that 43 per cent of the boarders had parents who jointly had no experience of boarding themselves. Indeed, of the fathers who had boarded, about a third were sending their sons to private schools as day boys.

These findings are in general agreement with information gained from a study I conducted in 1982 of one of the major HMC boarding schools (Walford, 1986a: 53). In a sample of about 200, only 45 per cent of the fathers had been boarders, and only 52 per cent had been to private schools. The figure for mothers was even lower, as only 26 per cent of mothers had boarded as girls. These figures are slightly higher than those found by Fox, indicating that there may be a greater degree of continuity between fathers and sons in the more elite schools than for the HMC as a whole. Nevertheless, both sets of data show a surprising degree of openness to new 'first generation' boys. The close contact that many of these families had with the maintained sector also suggests that decisions about which sector of education to use may well be informed decisions where parents are exercising genuine choice.

The study conducted by the Oxford Social Mobility Study can give us some information on the social class origins of boys in various types of private schools (Halsey *et al.*, 1980). The survey covered some 8,000 men who were born between 1913 and 1952, so the data are now rather old, and cover an extended period. Over the whole of this time only just over 500 of these men were educated in the private sector; thus, even though the educational system changed markedly during this period, it is only statistically meaningful to look at the group as a whole rather than in age cohorts. There are some fascinating and unexpected findings. For example, it was found that as many as 30 per cent of HMC boys had spent their primary education in the state sector. This is a considerable challenge to the accepted view that preparatory school is essential. In writing about social class Halsey *et al.* (1980) usually use a threefold scheme of service class (about 13 per cent of the respondents), inter-mediate class (about 30 per cent), and working class (about 56 per cent). They found that 67 per cent of HMC pupils came from the service class, 27 per cent came from the intermediate class, and there were even 6 per cent form the working class. This is a much higher degree of openness than is generally accepted to be the case, and is not very different from the figures for the direct grant schools, which often acted as local grammar schools, which are shown in table 4. Halsey *et al.* (1980) are at pains to point out that this evidence by itself does not necessarily mean that the system as a whole was not meritocratic. However, they construct a series of statistical models of selection and argue that class bias had an important part to play in which type of school was attended.

Table 4 Class composition of the different types of private school (%)

Father's class	HMC	Direct grant	Non-HMC
Service	67	50	48
Intermediate	27	34	41
Working	6	16	11

Source. Halsey *et al.* (1980): 53.

There is no available research which looks at the parental histories of girls in private schools. The best guess is that these schools are likely to have a higher proportion of 'first generation' pupils than the HMC schools. It is highly unlikely that they would be less open than the group of schools which has traditionally been regarded as the most socially closed and selective.

Why do parents use private schools?

There are surprisingly few research data available on why parents are prepared to spend large amounts of money on their children's education when they could receive it free in a state maintained school. A buoyant market has meant that most of the schools have not had to concern themselves too greatly with the problem, and politicians appear to believe that the answer to the question is too obvious to require stating.

Fox's work provides the most reliable answers but, of course, they relate only to the HMC parents that she studied. As might be expected, the reasons vary according to the family's educational background. For those 10 per cent of her sample where private education was simply a part of the general culture of the home, parents gave little thought to any alternative to the private system. A further 9 per cent of the parents could be said to have had a generalized belief that in using private education they were 'doing their best' for their sons, but they did not have clearly articulated reasons for such a choice. Fox then identifies a further 8 per cent who gave a large number of different reasons, 3 per cent who were so firmly against comprehensive education that no clear positive reasons were identifiable, and 4 per cent with boarding need. Altogether, this third of the sample had such a commitment to the private sector that further analysis was not possible.

Of much more interest, though, are the other two-thirds who gave clear reasons for their choice. Fox divides the remainder into three, somewhat overlapping, categories. Twenty-eight per cent had reasons classifiable as 'get on better in life', 23 per cent believed that such schools would provide academic advantage, and a further 14 per cent were concerned that the schools should 'develop character and foster discipline'. Those who believed that the schools could help their sons 'get on in life' often had a specific future in mind for them. Academic achievement was part of this, but these parents also wanted additional benefits such as character building and discipline, 'polish', or contacts. The 23 per cent who put academic advantage first were less likely to have a specific future mapped out for their son, and the academic results could be viewed as an end in themselves. For the parents of boarders, boarding was not a primary consideration, for fewer than 10 per cent of them gave desire for boarding as the sole or main reason for choosing a public school. The majority of parents of boarders believed that there were benefits to be gained from boarding, but that these were in addition to the benefits listed by the day parents. In sum, the most frequently mentioned reasons were the ability to produce better academic results and to develop the character by instilling discipline. Both these aspects were also seen to be of major importance by the boys questioned in my own study of a major boarding school (Walford, 1986a: 56).

A more recent study of the reasons that parents give for using the private sector was published by Johnson (1987). In terms of the research methods used, it is far less satisfactory than the work of Fox. Johnson's research concentrates on two local education authorities in the south-east of England. Twenty-five families were interviewed but, rather than being a random sample, they were selected from eighty-five responses to advertisements placed in the local press. Parents who had used both the private sector and the state sector for their children were invited to contact the author, giving details of their experiences. Those interviewed were chosen chiefly on the basis of the variety of patterns of use which the responses had revealed. This specifically chosen group from a self-selected sample thus cannot be regarded as representative in any way. Those with an axe to grind are bound to be predominate. In eleven of the families one or both of the parents was working as a teacher or had done so in the past. The selection of parents is such that most of them might be called 'refugees' from the state system, and Johnson presents a series of reports of bad experiences with the state sector. These reports are then discussed as if their validity is unquestionable.

While there are severe problems with Johnson's work, it remains worth studying for the range of reasons given for transfer from the state to the private sector. Perceived lack of suitable provision was one of the main causes of concern. The decline in the number of grammar schools and the demise of the direct grant schools were specifically cited, with the associated idea that comprehensive schools did not offer an adequate education to children with high academic ability. Academic success was of major importance to these parents. Johnson also found a group similar to that found by Fox who had a tradition of private school use. Another group had an almost unquestioned belief that fee-paying education was 'bound to be better', and yet another group specifically needed or wanted boarding for their children. Others of the parents reported a range of problems with maintained primary or secondary schools, some of which could be seen as part of a concern for discipline and character building. In general, however, this theme comes through less strongly in Johnson's study.

In a study conducted by MORI for Gabbitas Truman & Thring (1987), however, discipline emerged as one of the most highly rated perceived attributes of private schools. In October 1987 MORI questioned 309 parents with recent or current experience of having a child at an independent school. The parents were selected on a quota basis, using thirty-five constituency sampling points where there were known to be above-average incidence of upper- and middle-class households. The majority of questions required respondents to indicate their opinion about aspects of private education on a five-point scale. The research methods used in obtaining the sample and replies have limitations, but the results should at least be representative of the group studied.

The survey found that parents generally held private schools in high esteem. When asked to rate the schools' ability to 'encourage a responsible attitude to schoolwork', 77 per cent stated that it was 'very good'. The same rating was given by 66 per cent for 'discipline', by 62 per cent for 'size of classes', and by 62 per cent for 'exam results'. When choosing between private schools these parents stated that their priorities were discipline (60 per cent giving this a high priority), class sizes (55 per cent), the encouragement of a responsible attitude towards school work (50 per cent), and the reputation of the school (46 per cent). Surprisingly, the level of school fees, whether the school was single-sex or co-educational, or the social background of the children were all found to be relatively unimportant issues for this particular group of parents.

All the research discussed so far has been concerned with parents of children actually in private schools or considering their use. It is thus not unexpected that these parents should generally have had a high opinion of the schools. National polls of all parents indicate that the belief that private schools can offer advantages is widespread. A MORI poll for *Reader's Digest* in 1988, for example, found that 48 per cent of parents would consider sending their children to independent schools if they could afford to do so, while only 42 would not do so. Although three-quarters were satisfied with their children's maintained schools, some 20 per cent were not. Perceptions of lack of discipline and a growth in violence at school were widespread among parents, with 38 per cent being concerned nationally and 50 per cent in rural areas. It was shown in chapter two that the annual British Social Attitudes Survey shows a generally high level of support for the continued existence of private schools, which is consistent with these findings.

Do private schools give what parents want?

It has been shown above that there is considerable agreement about the advantages that parents believe they can obtain by using private education. This agreement extends beyond those parents with children in private schools to include those who use state maintained schools. Broadly, the main areas where parents believe that advantage can be bought are academic results, 'getting on', and 'development of character through discipline'. They believe that the academic ethos of these schools is such that their children will be encouraged to work hard for their examinations, which will enable them to enter university and, in turn, lead to secure and well paid careers. They also hope that the schools will have a positive moral impact on the children, and will encourage the development of maturity and culturally appropriate behaviour and interests. The next sections discuss the important question of the extent to which these schools live up to the image that parents have of them. It should also be recognized that there may well be other reasons for choosing private education which parents are less willing to admit in interview or on a questionnaire. The desire not to have a child mix with children from the local council housing estate, or with children from minority ethnic backgrounds, may be important for some parents, but is not likely to be readily endorsed publicly. This aspect is also briefly discussed.

Examination results

Halsey *et al.* (1984) compare the O-level and A-level examination results of the private and maintained sectors over the period 1961–81. They show that the maintained sector increased its share of the certificates at both levels, but that there was a significant exception.

> Despite its falling share of successful candidates the private sector managed to hold its own in the competition for three or more A levels – the crucial competition for university entry. The private schools produced 29 per cent of those obtaining three or more A levels in 1981 despite the fact that in the previous twenty years their share of the pupils aged 17+ fell from 29 per cent to 19 per cent.
>
> [Halsey *et al.*, 1984: 23]

In 1961 only two-fifths of leavers from private schools had any A levels at all, but by 1981 63 per cent were leaving with at least one A level, and 45 per cent had three or more. The state sector rather than the private sector had gained a greater share of both O-level and A-level examination successes, but this was simply because the relevant age group of pupils grew during this period at a greater rate than did the number in private schools. In the vital area of success in three or more A levels the private schools held their own. By 1986 21 per cent of 17-year-olds at school were back in the private sector and 63 per cent of all private school leavers obtained at least one A level and 46.4 per cent had three or more. The A-level results for all schools are shown in table 5.

In terms of university entry, it is the chance of gaining three or more A levels which is important. Since 1961 the chance of gaining three A levels from a private school, compared with the chance from a state maintained school, became more unequal. This is shown in table 6.

Privatization and privilege in education

Table 5 A-level results of all school leavers, 1987 (%)

	% attempting A levels	1 or 2 A levels	3+ A levels	No. of leavers
Private schools	66.3	16.7	46.4	44,630
Maintained schools	15.5	6.3	7.4	673,600

Source. DES (1987).

Table 6 Chances of obtaining three or more A levels in state and private schools, 1961–86

	% of school leavers with three or more A levels					
School	1961	1966	1971	1976	1981	1986
State	3.1	5.4	6.5	6.5	7.1	7.4
Private (including direct grant)	19.6	26.2	34.1	38.7	45.3	46.4
Odds ratio	7.6	6.2	7.4	9.1	10.8	10.7

Source. Based on Halsey *et al.* (1984: 26) and DES (1987)

There is a clear pattern of growing inequality here, although the 1986 figures tend to indicate that a plateau has been reached – nearly half of all private school leavers now obtain three or more A levels. But even this degree of inequality does not necessarily mean that it is unjust. To describe the number of certificates obtained by pupils in each of the two sectors does not answer the question of whether the private schools are actually more effective than maintained schools. Crudely, what comes out is related to what goes in. The better A-level results obtained in the private sector may well be attributable to background factors such as social class or measured intelligence, as well as to school-related factors such as teacher quality, staff–pupil ratios, or facilities. Parents often make the assumption that it is these school-related factors which lead to the better A-level results, but it may well be that it is the background factors that are more important. The pattern of growing inequality shown in table 5 could be due simply to proportionately more parents with educationally advantageous background characteristics sending their children to these schools. It is also worth re-emphasizing the diversity of the private sector (as well as the maintained sector) at this point. These very good examination success rates are not uniformly distributed throughout the private sector schools, so that the pupils in the leading schools achieve results which are far in excess of the average. Pupils in schools at the bottom of the hierarchy do far worse than the average maintained school.

One way of attempting to move beyond the descriptive to the explanatory is to postulate possible causes and then test out various models

46

of influence against empirical data. The ideal would be to control for these possible causes statistically to see how many of the observed differences can be attributed to each of the variables. Needless to say, there are no data available which allow this sort of analysis to be conducted on the full range of possible variables. While still having limitations, by far the most comprehensive data available are those collected by the Oxford Social Mobility Group in 1972 (Halsey *et al*. 1980, 1984; Goldthorpe, 1980). As already mentioned, they interviewed in depth a representative sample of about 8,000 men between the ages of 20 and 60, resident in England and Wales, and gathered data for family, educational, and occupational biographies. The data thus relate to men born between 1913 and 1952 and thus inevitably suffer from the main problem with any research of this kind – it can document and partially explain how the educational system worked in the past, but it can only give suggestions as to how it might be working now or in the future. This particular study also has the further disadvantage that it gives information only on men's and boy's schools. Gross average figures for all the sample would conceal the very real changes that occurred in education over the forty-year period, so here we will only examine the last of these cohorts, who were born in the period 1943–52.

Halsey *et al*. (1984) constructed three statistical models which incorporate different assumptions. When tested against the data collected, all three indicate that school-related variables had an effect on the examination performance of this cohort of pupils. These men were in the sixth forms of their schools during the 1960s, and by this time pupils with similar backgrounds, and staying on at school for the same length of time, were more likely to get at least one A-level pass in the private sector than in the state maintained sector. In other words, pupils with the same background characteristics did better in the private sector. The difference was small but significant, and was in contrast to what had been found for earlier cohorts, where the choice did not seem to be significant. A more detailed analysis, which looked at the diversity of schools to be found in both the maintained and the private sectors, showed that in the 1960s the direct grant schools had a lead over the HMC schools (in terms of the advantage given to pupils from similar family backgrounds and staying on for the same length of time), with the grammar schools and non-HMC private schools trailing badly. As Halsey *et al*. (1984: 31) point out:

> This is an important result. It suggests that the rise in the relative success of the private sector predates comprehensive reorganisation. In the period we are considering, the 1960s, it would still have been the grammar schools which catered for the growing numbers of sixth formers within the state sector, and it was against this competition

from grammar schools that the private sector was already beginning to pull ahead.

Patterns of numerical associations between variables do not, of themselves, provide answers to questions as to how the direct grant and HMC schools achieved their advantage. Halsey *et al.* suggested three possibilities: the differences could be due to increased academic selectivity; genuine 'school effects' in terms of better teaching or facilities; or they could be an unintended consequence of larger sixth forms, which generate, through increased competition, better pupil attitudes and motivation. They suggested that, while all three might be necessary for a full explanation, they would be inclined to put more weight on the first explanation of greater selectivity and least on actual school variables. They argued that, while they were able to take account of family background in their analysis, they did not have information on measured intelligence or on the educational ambitions of parents. Greater selectivity according to these and other 'unmeasured' variables could account for much of the difference in performance.

From the parents' point of view, this explanation is unhelpful, for these background characteristics are exactly the ones which cannot be changed, no matter how much money is spent. If the advantage that private schools appear to give is actually due to increased selectivity, then the parents' money spent on private schools is wasted. If the child is academically able enough to be selected, then he or she is good enough to get just as many A levels in a maintained school. However, while Halsey *et al.* put most weight on this explanation, they also admitted that the other two reasons might have an effect. It is left to the parent to judge how much that extra effect may be worth in cash terms.

University and higher education entry

While the Oxford Social Mobility data do benefit from a wide range of information available and sophisticated analysis, the data collected are now growing old and are restricted to men only. There are no comparable data on A-level examination successes, but some data on university entry have recently been made available through a study conducted for the Department of Education and Science. Redpath and Harvey (1987) were responsible for a survey concerned with young people's intentions to enter higher education, which was conducted by the Office of Population Censuses and Surveys (OPCS) in late 1985 and early 1986. The sample was based on students taking A levels or BTEC National/OND/ONC examinations in June 1985 at 485 randomly selected schools and colleges in England and Wales. Those who were not in higher education were interviewed either by telephone or face-to-face, while those in higher education were sent questionnaires. Over 6,000 replies were received. The overall response rate of 74 per cent was influenced considerably by some schools which would not fully co-operate owing to concern about confidentiality. Where schools did co-operate fully a high response rate of 85 per cent was achieved. The data were reweighted to take account of a shortfall in replies from further education colleges. It is evident that the study was well conducted, and the findings have good generalizability.

The general findings about application rates are unexceptional. Students from private schools had higher application rates to higher education, particularly to universities, than did students from maintained schools, who, in turn, had higher application rates than students from further education. This finding is in agreement with an earlier small-scale study by Eglin (1984), and could be simply related to the social class composition of the users of the two sectors. The acceptance rates followed the same pattern, with proportionally more pupils from private schools being accepted for higher education and for universities than pupils from maintained schools.

The study produced far more unexpected results when social class was taken into account. It is well known that boys and girls from social classes I and II are far more likely than those from other social class backgrounds to have attended private school, to obtain more and higher-grade A-level results, and to enter university. However, Redpath and Harvey found that if they took children from social class I backgrounds and compared those who attended private schools with those who went to maintained schools, there was no difference in higher education application rates or attainment rates for their sample of pupils (already taking A level or equivalent examinations). Table 7 shows that the proportion of social class I background pupils (from A-level or equivalent sixth forms) who went on to higher education after attending maintained schools was actually slightly higher than the proportion from private schools.

Table 7 Entry to higher education, according to social class of head of household and type of institution previously attended (%)

	Social class I		Social class II		III + IV + V	
	Private	*State*	*Private*	*State*	*Private*	*State*
At university or deferred entry	47	49	48	35	41	32
At polytechnic	11	14	16	18	21	21
At other PSHE institution	10	10	8	11	11	11
Qualified but not in higher education	26	19	20	23	19	22
Not qualified	6	8	8	13	8	14
Base N = 100%	178	294	349	1,013	136	844

Source. Based on Redpath and Harvey (1987).

The figures given refer only to those sixth-form pupils who actually applied to enter higher education, but in addition to the fact that social class I pupils from maintained schools had a higher chance of entry, they were also more likely to apply than those educated in private schools. In all, 87 per cent of the social class I maintained school group applied to enter higher education, while 84 per cent of the corresponding private school-educated group did so. In terms of entry to university, it would thus appear that these professional and managerial parents may have wasted their money by using the private sector for their children once they had entered the sixth form. Having obtained sufficient O-levels to enter the sixth form, the chances are that these boys and girls might have done just as well, if not better, in the maintained sector.

This is not true for children with other social class backgrounds. For those from social class II the application rate for the private sector was 82 per cent, compared with 78 per cent from the state schools. Once an application had been made the chance of acceptance was also higher, substantially so for universities, where 48 per cent of private school applicants were accepted but only 35 per cent of maintained school applicants. This advantage also applies to children from the remaining social class groups, where the application rate was 69 per cent for the maintained sector and 77 per cent for the private sector. Table 7 shows that the acceptance rates again differed considerably, with 41 per cent of private school applicants obtaining a university place, against 32 per cent of those from the maintained sector.

Redpath and Harvey (1987) also considered in detail the effect of a parent having a degree. They show that for these sixth-form pupils, where one or both parents have a degree (or higher qualification), there was no difference in either the higher education application or the acceptance rates between those attending maintained or private schools. This is another quite unexpected finding, but none of this necessarily means that private education is a bad investment either for graduate parents or for those from social class I. It must be remembered that these results apply only to those who had already embarked upon sixth-form study, and the initial staying-on rate for private schools is far higher than for maintained schools. Although this information is not available according to social class, it is likely that children from social class I in private schools were far more likely to stay on than those in the maintained sector. The slightly lower application rates and acceptance rates may well be more than compensated for by the higher chance of entering the sixth form. Neither does it mean that financially prudent parents should necessarily opt into the maintained sector once A levels have been decided upon, for the further education colleges, which are among the most likely choices for students, have a significantly lower higher education application and acceptance rate than either the private or maintained schools.

Redpath and Harvey (1987) did not consider the divisions within the private sector in any of their calculations, and there is no other data set which allows this sort of detailed analysis to be tackled. However, it is worth noting that the higher education entry rates differ considerably between school associations. In 1987, 62 per cent of HMC school leavers went on to higher education (46 per cent into universities), 32 per cent of SHMIS leavers did so (15 per cent into universities), as did 46 per cent of GBA/GBGSA leavers (31 per cent into university) and 16 per cent of ISAI leavers (8 per cent into university). These figures relate to all leavers aged 15 and above, so that those girls who transferred from GSA/GBGSA schools to HMC schools are counted in the HMC totals. Nevertheless, the variation illustrates the fallacy of assuming that attendance at a private school, no matter which, automatically ensures entry to higher education.

Although entry to any university is a considerable achievement, it is generally recognized that some universities are harder to enter than others. Oxford and Cambridge, in particular, require very high entry grades. In 1981, for example, nearly three-quarters of students accepted had thirteen points or more in A levels (i.e. AAC grades or better). In 1963 the Robbins Committee concluded that for both Oxford and Cambridge there was evidence that the average qualifications of male entrants from the maintained sector were better than those from the HMC boarding schools, and that these private students achieved fewer first-class degrees and more third-class degrees than those from the maintained schools. At that time the connections between individual private schools and some Oxbridge colleges clearly enabled less well qualified pupils to enter. The Franks Report (1966) for Oxford supported these findings.

Both universities have since made considerable efforts to overcome this inequality and to make it easier for state maintained pupils to apply. The Dover Report (1983) on Oxford showed that the situation had certainly improved, but that there remained some differences to be accounted for. In 1983 there were 5,870 people in Britain who achieved an A-level score of thirteen points or more, 39 per cent of whom were from the private sector. Oxford took 51 per cent of its intake from the private sector that year. Although this is a major difference, it does not necessarily show that the selection procedures are unfair, for it may be that high-scoring applicants from the maintained sector prefer to go to other universities. We do not have the data to tell (Halsey *et al.*, 1984).

Richie (1988) reports a similar concern with the entry standards of private school-educated students at Edinburgh University. It was found in 1984 that the average A-level score for English private school entrants to the social sciences was 11.78, compared with 12.54 points for English state school entrants. Further significant differences were found within the other faculties. In this case it appeared that private school students taking an extra year to prepare for Oxbridge entrance examinations, or taking a year off after A level, were gaining an advantage simply because they were being offered unconditional places on the basis of their existing A-level grades. Some conditional offers were higher entry grades than these students had achieved.

'Getting on' in society

There are now several studies which show that current members of a variety of elites in society are disproportionately likely to have been educated privately. The major study is that of Boyd (1973), who looked at high-ranking members of the civil service, the judiciary, the armed forces, the clergy, and the clearing banks. He found an overwhelming predominance of ex-public school boys in these top positions. Reid (1986) collected similar more recent evidence on the same groups and on those in elite positions in commerce, industry, and politics. The picture for the 1980s is still very similar to that found by Boyd in the early 1970s – there is a very high chance that members of present-day elites went to private schools. For example, 89 per cent of law lords, 69 per cent of ambassadors, a somewhat reduced 50 per cent of top civil servants, 92 per cent of directors of major clearing banks, 70 per cent of Conservative MPs and even 14 per cent of Labour MPs came from private schools.

Such data might well encourage parents to believe that using a private school is likely to give a great boost to the chance that their child will 'get on' in society. As explained earlier, such a conclusion is not necessarily justified, for there are three fundamental problems. The first is the now familiar one that although these elite members attended private schools, such attendance may have been simply a cultural accompaniment of the social class from which they were drawn. Their social backgrounds may well have been such that, in our class-dominated society, they would have risen to the top of their professions whether or not they had attended private schools.

The second problem is that the number of schools represented by the members of such elites is actually very limited. Only a very few schools provide the majority of such elite members. Practically all were educated in HMC schools rather than any other group of private schools. In fact, even this category is artificially wide, for it is predominantly the boarding schools which have schooled present elite members. Within this group, schools such as Harrow and Eton dominate. At least 40 per cent of MPs in 1982 were educated in HMC schools, but 20 per cent of these were from Eton (Walford, 1986a: 13). Thus it is not that these elite members attended private schools, but that they attended a few select private schools, which is important.

52

Schools within the Rugby and Eton Groups are significantly over-represented.

The third problem is that while it is possible to gather information on the schooling of people at present in elite groups or in professional occupations and calculate the percentage who had a private school background, it is obviously impossible to find out what careers present pupils will eventually take up. We thus know only something about the relationship between occupations now and private school attendance often some forty or more years ago – which may be very different from the similar relationship for pupils now in private schools. To make the point once again, hardly any of the members of elites at present are women, but we can certainly expect that there will be many more by the time present students rise to eminence.

Boyd and others also demonstrate that attendance at university, in particular Oxford and Cambridge, was of considerable importance. The private schools may be correct in emphasizing their Oxbridge successes, for it would seem that this is a slightly more important attribute than public school attendance alone in predicting those in elite positions. Entry into Oxbridge has now become practically entirely meritocratic. Some major schools may be able to gain some advantages for their pupils simply because they are more knowledgeable about the admission system, but the applicants must still obtain the required very high level of A-level successes to be admitted. Thus we can expect that any advantage that privte schools now have in this first stage of 'getting on' in society is very highly correlated with their ability to encourage good A levels, and thus university entry.

Entry into professional occupations is also now mainly dependent upon academic achievement, especially at Oxbridge, and for some professions a 'public school accent' is a distinct disadvantage. But a successful career demands more than just entry to it. To rise to the top of a chosen profession demands particular social and interpersonal skills and abilities, contacts, hard work, and single-minded determination. This, of course, is closely related to parents' desire that schools develop 'character by instilling discipline'. Do the trends indicate any increase or decrease in the ability of the private schools to develop these attributes?

Discipline and character building

It is in this area of parents' expectations about private schools that there is possibly the most variation between schools. It seems reasonable to assume that the ethos of a 'typical' HMC boarding school (if there is such a thing) is bound to be very different from that of a GSA/GBGSA school or from that of one in membership of ISAI. One would expect a boarding school to differ significantly from a day school, and those in the country differ from those in the heart of urban areas. However, this is a topic where generalizable information is very difficult to find, and what exists is usually out of date.

One of the difficulties is that the desire which many parents have that the schools should 'develop the character through discipline' is very ill defined. For the parents of boys in traditional HMC schools in 1979/80 Fox (1984: 57) claims that:

> What parents require of the schools is that they impose discipline upon their children, teaching them what is right and wrong, to dress properly and ultimately to develop a tidy mind and self-discipline in order that they can learn to live in a world which has rules.

She adds that, in the majority of cases, this idea of the development of character through discipline bears little resemblance to the service to the community that Lambert (1975) sees as central to the public school ethos. Likewise, she found that preparation for leadership and the development of a sense of responsibility were mentioned by very few of the parents. Yet many of the HMC schools make elaborate claims to be educating the 'whole person' and to not just be concerned about narrow academic success. The prospectuses of schools make it clear that a whole range of what Lambert (1975) has catalogued as 'expressive goals' are to be seen as an essential part of the educational process.

Training for leadership has been a major part of the public school tradition, and is an essential part of 'getting on' in life. Wilkinson (1964) argues that British government has been dominated by a gentleman elite trained to public leadership in the public schools. He views the public schools as a political institution, nourishing the power of a gentleman class and indoctrinating it with distinctive manners and binding loyalties, and shows that there was a marked similarity between the values and mechanisms of public school society and those of British government. He sees the 'character building' which took place in public schools as an ideal educational device for maintaining a public servant elite. Whilst parents may not actually use the term 'leadership', it seems inevitable that many of them still look for these qualities.

I have argued elsewhere (Walford, 1986b) that the last two decades have seen considerable changes in many aspects of life in the major HMC schools, the most significant of which is the shift towards the pre-eminence of academic work. The increasing need for high qualifications to enter higher education has forced the schools to put academic goals before almost all others. There has thus been a corresponding decrease in the emphasis given to other activities. Sporting activities and team games no longer hold a great power over most pupils, the Combined Cadet Force has faded greatly in importance, as have chapel and religion. Older pupils now seem less inclined to play a major part in the organization of the younger boys in the Houses, and the claims of work are more frequently heard to be in conflict with prefectorial duties or playing sport for the House or the school. The schools have become more like 'exam mills', and with this trend has come a move away from educating the 'whole person' and 'building the character'. The leading schools may well have become very efficient at obtaining certification for their pupils and gaining them entry into higher education. However, it may be that, once university entry has been gained, these public school pupils will be now less well equipped to 'get on' in their chosen professional occupation than previously.

Before moving on to discuss other privileges which attendance at private school may bring, it is worth considering some of the features of private education which parents may well actually want, but are not likely to wish to make too public. The first is that attendance at a private school is not open to all children. Most parents have to pay high fees for their children, and such payment ensures that their child will mix only with other children of parents willing and able to pay. Parents can be sure, for example, that there will be very few poor working-class children in the school for their own child to interact with and be influenced by. The only possibility of children from poor families will be those highly selected pupils on scholarships or assisted places, who are likely to be seen as a potentially good influence rather than bad. Private education also gives the opportunity for parents to choose a school which has few, if any, children from ethnic minorities. The number of West Indian children, in particular, is very low in practically all British private schools. It is obviously impossible to estimate how important this aspect might be, for parents are unlikely to admit to this particular preference, but social exclusiveness is obviously regarded by some as a privilege which can be bought at these schools.

Privilege while at school?

British sociology of education has traditonally been concerned with charting inequalities of opportunity and outcomes. Most academic discussion of the private sector has thus emphasized the inegalitarian intakes to private schools and the way in which wealthy parents are able to buy better future life chances for their children by using these schools. Yet, for the children who go to private schools, about one-sixth of their entire lives will be dominated by that choice. Most sociologists seem to have forgotten that the years between 5 and 18 are important in themselves, apart from how they will affect the following sixty or so years of life. In what ways may private education actually make life more enjoyable for pupils?

While there may be a limited number of children who enjoy hard work for its own sake, most children do not, yet they often still find at least something to enjoy at school. For many, it is simply the social activities with other children which the structure of schooling allows them to take part in. Many pupils also enjoy sporting activities and using the specialized facilities provided by schools, while for some others it is drama, music, or art which have a special fascination. Within the private sector, what individual schools offer in these areas is extremely varied, with some schools virtually excluding these 'extra-curricular' areas altogether. At the top end, however, privilege can certainly be bought.

In the sample of boys questioned in one of the major HMC boarding schools 28 per cent stated that they 'thoroughly enjoyed being here' and a further 46 per cent said they 'had a reasonably pleasant time here' (Walford,1986a: 59). It was clear that the great range of sporting and artistic facilities that were available to them were a major part of this enjoyment, and several of the boys claimed that boarding rather than day had been their choice, rather than the choice of their parents, because they believed that they would enjoy it more.

It is easy to see why many boys might have an enjoyable time. Take Rugby, for example, where just over 700 pupils have 8 squash courts, 6 fives courts, 12 grass tennis courts and 9 hard tennis courts at their disposal. There is also a gymnasium, swimming bath, and playing fields covering 86 acres. Pupils can take part in 23 different sports. For those more interested in 'creative arts' there are separate studios for painting and drawing, for pottery and sculpture, and a photographic darkroom, and a craft workshop. The school has its own modern theatre, with more than 20 pupil productions each year. For music, there are 25 rooms for instrumental practice, two Steinway concert grand pianos, and three organs. The school has eight full-time music teachers who between them teach all the orchestral instruments. These facilities are typical of those available in the Rugby and Eton Group schools, and contrast sharply with what is available in most maintained schools, and with the facilities of the cheaper private schools. As Griggs (1985: 70) argues, 'sports halls, which seem to go beyond the resources of many towns, have sprung up in the building boom within the private schools'.

Table 8 gives an indication of the amount of money spent on new buildings, improvements to buildings, and equipment in the last five years. The data were obtained from successive issues of the ISIS Annual Census, and the amounts are not corrected for inflation. To some extent these average figures are confusing, for they include both day and boarding schools. Some of both the new buildings and the improvements to buildings will be related to the boarding side; thus it is likely that boarding schools will be above the average presented here, with day schools below. The mix between day and boarding within an association will affect the average given, which may well account for the

Table 8 Average expenditure per year per pupil on buildings and equipment, 1985–7 (£)

	HMC	SHMIS	GBA	GSA/ GBGSA	IAPS	ISAI	All schools
New buildings	229	293	138	153	143	77	171
Improvements to buildings and equipment	163	148	108	83	75	50	106

seemingly generous provision for new buildings SHMIS schools, where more than half the pupils are boarders. Nevertheless, an interesting pattern emerges, where boys obtain more than girls and older pupils more than younger pupils. It is also worth recognizing that as the majority of this is capital expenditure rather than current, the differences between the associations cumulates. Each year the difference widens between the buildings and facilities available in the average boys' school and the average girls' school. The dramatic difference between spending in the GSA/GBGSA schools (where 21 per cent board) and the HMC schools (where 30 per cent board) cannot be accounted for in terms of the different proportion of boarders. It is simply that those schools which already have very good facilities seem to be spending even more.

While the major schools are able to offer excellent facilities, the smaller and poorer ones are often far worse-off than most state maintained schools. Lodge (1987), for example, reports on a survey of sports facilities which found that the private school sector as a whole, which caters for 7 per cent of the school population, had only 5 per cent of the total playing field area used by educational establishments. Golf was almost three times more likely to be available as an option at a state school than at a private one. State schools were also slightly ahead overall in terms of tennis courts and hockey pitches. On the other hand, 83 per cent of private schools had their own athletics track, compared with 57 per cent of maintained schools, and there is evidence that the private sports facilities may be in better condition – the groundsmen use at least twice as much fertilizer per acre than in the state sector!

While good leisure facilities at the major schools give pupils a better chance of enjoying their years at school, so do the facilities designed for academic study. Irrespective of whether or not new science laboratories, craft, design, and technology centres, and computer centres actually lead to more and better qualifications, they are surely more enjoyable to be in and use. To be able to use a good microcomputer individually is bound to be more fun than sharing an outdated one between four pupils. A survey in 1985 showed that there was one computer per

260 pupils in maintained schools, against one to twenty-six pupils in private schools (Ginn, 1987). Both these figures will have considerably improved since then, but it is most unlikely that the difference will have been removed.

The quality and number of staff at the schools are also likely to have a large effect on pupils' happiness. Poor-quality teaching staff not only hinder a child's chances of obtaining good GCSEs and A levels, but also make school less enjoyable. A teacher who is lively and fun, yet clear and organized in teaching, makes a pupil's life far more enjoyable than one who is worn-out and muddled. The major HMC and GSA/GBGSA schools are able to be highly selective in their choice of teachers. They are able to choose staff who, in addition to being academically well qualified, have a range of other interests and activities to add to school life. The major schools are able to fix their salary scale and the salaries of individual teachers such that good teachers can be attracted and retained. A survey of thirty private schools conducted by the interim advisory body for teachers' pay in 1988 (Sutcliffe 1988b) found that many were paying well above the Baker scale. One was paying about £5,000 more and another nearly £4,000 more. Most were paying about the same as the Baker scale, with about a third paying between 2 and 5 per cent more. Teachers in girls' schools were generally paid less than teachers in boys' schools. It is also fairly easy for headmasters of private schools to 'ease out' teachers who do not come up to standard. Note, however, that the same survey found that one school was paying £440 less than the Baker scale, and, while money is not the only attraction to teaching in the private sector, it is likely that this school had far less room for choice in its teachers.

Not only is it likely that the highest-ranking schools will have more able teachers than those in the maintained sector, it is also likely that they will have more of them. In 1987 the pupil/teacher ratio for maintained primary schools was 21.9 : 1, while it was 15.5 : 1 for maintained secondary schools (DES, 1988). In 1988 HMC schools had an average of 11.6 teaching staff for every pupil, GSA/GBGSA schools 11.4, SHMIS schools 10.3 and ISAI schools 12.7. Even at the prep. school level IAPS schools had one teacher for every 11.6 children. I have argued elsewhere (Walford, 1986a) that these figures are not quite as good as they seem , for a there is a higher proportion of sixth-form pupils in private schools who require more specialized teaching. In boarding schools there is the additional factor that these same teachers are involved in managing sporting, boarding, and entertainment activities for pupils, which takes a considerable portion of their working time, but the ratios still appear to be better than in most maintained schools.

The main advantage of the low pupil/teacher ratios is that classes can be smaller. While teachers continually press for smaller class sizes, strangely enough the research evidence in terms of improved academic performance is more mixed. The effects are small, and not always consistent. Within a range of reasonable possibilities, class size does not seem to make very much difference to academic results (Glass *et al.*, 1982). The advantage of smaller classes is in the classroom environment, which is likely to be friendlier and more conducive to learning. Teachers' morale is also higher, as they find teaching smaller classes easier and more fulfilling. Pupils also enjoy lessons in smaller classes more than in large classes.

Finally, it is worth recognizing that for some pupils the very fact of being away from home and their parents can make their lives more enjoyable. In the majority of cases this is not due to a particularly bad home life, but simply that some children enjoy the independent and full lives that a boarding school can offer. This is unlikely to be the case for many younger children, but by 13, and certainly by 15 or 16, many young people would enjoy time spent away from their parents. The boys from a major HMC boarding school who answered a question on the advantages of boarding gave a variety of replies (Walford, 1986a: 60). The most mentioned advantage they saw was that being away from home allowed them to be more independent. It got them away from what they often saw as the cloying and pervasive demands of their parents. At a simple level some boys wanted to 'get away from the old man' or just 'get away from parents'. The advantage was that 'you don't have to communicate with your parents if you don't want to', and it meant that 'parents don't nag at you all the time'. Many of the boys felt that being away from home positively improved their relationship with their parents; it had made holidays much more enjoyable than they would otherwise have been and reduced the number of arguments. These boys felt that the boarding aspect of being at one of the major schools improved their lives.

Not all boys and girls have such a positive experience of boarding, of course. While it would seem that most of these boarders were happy to be away from home for a while, some 10 per cent of the sample of boys in the study mentioned bullying or teasing as one of the problems they experienced (Walford, 1988d), and some of the younger boys reported homesickness. These bullies in boarding schools were unlikely to indulge in grossly violent behaviour – their activities might even be defined as 'joking' in another context. But in a closed environment, where just a few boys are sometimes picked out to receive such behaviour, it can mean that boarding becomes a punishment rather than a privilege for those who become the target of abuse.

Summary

The question of whether or not it is possible to purchase privilege through the private schools is more complicated than it appears. While it is easy to show that many of those who attended private schools in the past are now in positions of power and prestige, it is difficult to show that this success was in any way caused by school attendance. Further, while this can be shown to have been true in the past, it does not follow that a similar relationship will hold in the future for pupils currently in private schools.

The chapter shows that a large proportion of the parents of boys in HMC schools were not themselves privately educated. They appear to choose private schools for their children after comparing what is on offer in the state maintained sector. The most common reason for using private schools was a belief that the schools would produce better examination results and develop the character by instilling discipline. Recent research shows that the better schools are able to offer the advantage that these parents seek in terms of qualifications, but that they may be less effective than they were in terms of ensuring that pupils 'get on' in their chosen careers.

As the years between 5 and 18 are important in themselves as well as for their effect on future prospects, it is worth recognizing that the major private schools, at least, may offer considerable privileges for their pupils in terms of facilities and independence. In contrast, the cheaper schools may have far worse facilities than are available in most state maintained schools. Whether boarding as such is regarded as a privilege depends on the individual child and the family circumstances.

Chapter four

Privatization

Privatization has been one of the major policy priorities of the three Conservative governments since 1979. The broad ideology of privatization, which extols free-market capitalism and has faith in the natural efficiency of competition, has led to fundamental changes in the role of the state at the local and national levels. This chapter will first examine how the process of privatization has occurred at the general level, and then consider the ways in which changes within education can be seen as part of this wider process.

Privatization outside education

Privatization is a general term which has come to be applied to a number of apparently disparate government policies. The most obvious case of privatization is the sale of government-owned monopolies and trading companies to shareholders, but the range of areas where related privatization processes have occurred includes residential homes for the elderly, bus deregulation, the sale of council homes, pensions, health, and social services. In all these cases there has been a shift in what government sees as the desirable mix between private and state provision, and a greater degree of overlap between the two. Papadakis and Taylor-Gooby (1987) argue that in all cases there has been a reduction in the level of state provision (although not necessarily state subsidy), and a corresponding encouragement of the expansion of private provision. This has occurred in welfare services, providers of essential services (which were once regarded as being 'natural' monopolies), as well as manufacturing and service companies. Privatization, then, is not simply concerned with the direct sale of national assets.

This broad definition of privatization is accepted by Madsen Pirie (1985), who, writing in a pamphlet published by the right-wing Adam Smith Institute, suggested that privatization is a complex and subtle process which takes very different forms in each case. He sees it not as a fixed formula but as a general approach which can generate and focus policy ideas. He illustrates this diversity through a list of about twenty different methods by which privatization has been achieved. These range from selling the whole or part, charging for services, contracting out, buying out existing interest groups and repealing monopolies, to diluting the public sector, encouraging alternative institutions, encouraging exit from state institutions, and divestment. He then gives explicit examples where each method has been used, some of which will be discussed in the rest of this section.

Britain has not been alone in its growing support for private provision of social welfare, or in its rapid privatization of government-owned companies and service organizations. Largely similar trends are apparent in many of the other more developed countries as well (see, for example, Cameron, 1985; Mishra, 1984), and even in some of the less developed countries. But Britain has been one of those leading the way, and the dramatic pace of privatization has gathered more momentum here than practically anywhere else. The nature of these changes can be illustrated by taking three examples – the growth of private housing the contracting out of state-funded services, and the denationalization of public monopolies and other trading companies.

Housing

Papadakis and Taylor-Gooby (1987) show clearly that there is nothing new about state encouragement of private housing. Income tax payers buying their own homes on a mortgage, for example, have long been able to set the interest payable against tax. In addition, owner occupiers receive preferential treatment in the taxation of wealth, and numerous improvements are available for private owners of poor property. However, Margaret Thatcher's Conservative governments, by promoting the sale of council houses to tenants, have greatly increased the proportion of households in their own accommodation.

In 1914 only 10 per cent of the housing stock was owner-occupied and 90 per cent was privately rented. After the Second World War the amount of both council housing and owner occupied housing rapidly increased, reaching 29 per cent and 44 per cent respectively by 1971 (Papadakis and Taylor-Gooby, 1987: 138). The proportion of council housing was still at 29 per cent in 1981 when the effects of the sales began to have their effect. By 1984 the proportion was down to 26 per cent.

The sale of council houses has been permitted since 1925, but little encouragement had been given to tenants to buy until the introduction of the Conservatives' 1957 Housing Act, which allowed discounts of up to 20 per cent. During the 1970s some local authorities (usually those which were Conservative-controlled) had encouraged such sales, but the total number of council homes which had been transferred to the private sector was small. The extension of the 'right to buy' council housing was one of the more specific and popular of the Conservative Party's 1979 election promises. The 1980 Housing Act extended the rate of discount to up to 50 per cent of the market value and made it compulsory for councils to sell if the tenant wished to buy. To encourage the privatization process further, the maximum possible discount was raised to 60 per cent in the 1984 Act and to 70 per cent in 1986. The result is that between 1980 and 1986 nearly one million homes were sold to tenants at well below market prices. Most of these sales occurred during Margaret Thatcher's first term of office, but the pace of sales increased again in 1986 as the result of a rise in the maximum discount made available.

In the case of housing, the encouragement towards privatization was not simply a matter of subsidizing sales of council houses. That was the 'carrot', but the 'stick' was also in evidence. Since 1979 local authority spending has gradually become ever more strictly controlled by central government, such that, in real terms, public expenditure on housing was reduced by 45 per cent between 1979/80 and 1984/5. Council housing has thus become more difficult to obtain, forcing those without housing to enter an ever diminishing private rented sector or to take on what might be a highly burdensome mortgage. At the same time, the restrictions on local authority spending and specific government regulations have forced local councils to make substantial increases in rents for those remaining in council accommodation.

The overall result is that the council housing sector has shrunk, and the divisions between those in private housing and those in council housing have widened. About half of council tenants in 1985 were in receipt of rent rebates and supplementary benefits. Council housing has become more of a residual and socially distinct sector, providing poor-quality housing for the unemployed, the single-parent families, and for the poor and elderly. Meanwhile, those who have bought their homes have frequently seen the value of their property double in three or four years.

Contracting out

The second example of the process of privatization is that of contracting out of various social services which had previously been supplied direct by local or central government or by district health authorities. There had been some experimentation with contracting out such local authority services as refuse collection and architectural services in the late 1950s and 1960s, but the results had generally been found to be unsatisfactory, and by 1979 many of these services had been taken back into local council control. In a similar way, the use of contract catering in the National Health Service had declined from thirty-three contracts in 1965 to only two in 1984. However, the belief that efficiency was likely to be increased through competitive tendering for contracts led Mrs Thatcher's first government to quickly introduce an Act compelling local authorities to put building and road works out to tender. Local authorities were also encouraged to seek bids for other services such as refuse collection and street cleaning, but the response was very limited. Such lack of enthusiasm led to further legislation in 1988 which enforced compulsory competitive tendering for a range of local authority services, including refuse collection, public building and street cleaning, the maintenance of playing fields and parks, and all catering services.

The government also wished to see further privatization of the National Health Service through the increased use of contracting-out of laundry, cleaning, and catering services. In practice, the cancellation of earlier unsuccessful outside contracts in these areas led to a decrease in contracted-out spending in the first few years after 1979, such that the government was forced to issue a circular instruction the health authorities to open up cleaning, catering, and laundry services to outside agencies. The number of hospitals relying on private firms for major cleaning services rose from forty to over 100 between 1980 and 1985 (Ascher, 1987). Full privatization of health services was brought one stage nearer in 1989 with proposals to allow individual hospitals to opt out of local control and become self-managing.

There are several good reasons why in-house provision had developed in the public services. Ascher(1987) argues that the highly specialized and unusual nature of welfare and social services differentiates them from the more common commercial situations where private sub-contracting is much more commonly employed. There are three points to this. First, there is a need for public services to provide for clients in a fair and equitable way. Second, with some services, such as refuse collection or social work with children, there is a high level of risk involved if adequate standards of service are not maintained. The possibility of causing disease or death is a far more drastic possibility with failure of public services than usually occurs in the private sector. Third, it is often difficult in public services to specify what the 'outputs' should be in numerical terms. Contracting out requires standards of service to be tightly set, yet client satisfaction may depend on aspects which are generally unquantifiable.

The difficulty of specifying the level of service required is part of the reason for the mixed evidence so far on the degree of success of current contracting-out schemes. In many cases cost savings certainly have been made, but this may well be related to a cut in the quality of services provided. Alternatively, some savings have been made by reducing the wage rates of employees, or by worsening their conditions of service. For example, in order to ensure that outside employers were able to undercut the bids of groups of internal employees, the Fair Wage Resolution, which has stood since 1964, was abolished. This required the revoking of Convention 94 of the International Labour Organization (Rentoul, 1987). 'Efficiency savings' have, at least in part, often been the direct result of reductions in pay and conditions for workers – in particular those involved in low-paid manual labour, who are likely to be women or from ethnic minorities.

Sale of public monopolies and other trading companies

The third example of the process of privatization is the denationalization of public monopolies and other trading companies formerly under government ownership and control. Although often seen as being almost synonymous with the concept of privatization, this particular aspect was not a major feature of early Conservative government policy. The initial election promise concentrated on the denationalization of the aerospace and shipbuilding industries, which had recently been taken into public ownership by the previous Labour government (Rentoul, 1987). British Aerospace was sold in 1982 along with the National Freight Corporation, Amersham International, and part of Britoil. The last of these sales, which raised over £330 million, was the first privatization to bring into the Exchequer any significant income. This extra income was welcomed within a government becoming increasingly ideologically committed not only to privatization but also to the reduction of taxation. The sale of further state-owned industries was seen as a convenient way by which both these interests could be served. The calls of the far right for the government to privatize as much as possible of public provision, and to dispose of all trading concerns in government hands, could now be given more attention, with the added advantage of major additions to government revenue. The sums involved have been substantial, with, for example, British Telecom raising £4,000 million, and British Gas bringing in £5,000 million. In most of these cases, in order to ensure that the privatization could be seen as successful, shares in the new companies have been offered at a discount. Buyers have been offered a windfall profit, and the government has been able to claim that the privatization was enthusiastically welcomed by the public. The effect of such privatizations is, of course, to sell to a few people what had previously belonged to all. The windfall gains were available only to those with sufficient free cash to buy the shares, so there is a net transfer from the poor to the rich.

The ideology of privatization

In all these three areas, the underlying ideology of privatization is based upon the belief that the public sector is wasteful, inefficient, and unproductive, while the private sector is efficient, effective, and responsive to the rapid changes that are needed in the modern world. The public sector is seen as slow, unresponsive, and bureaucratic, while the competition of the private sector is seen as leading to 'value for money' for the consumer who is also seen to to benefit from a diversity of products and ways of delivering services to suit individual requirements. Privatization of the welfare services is not simply about perceived increased efficiency and value for money. The underlying ideology is a far deeper belief that privatization puts the clients and consumers in the position of customers, who are then able to choose between competing providers and producers. Customers are seen as having greater choice and power over the nature and content of provision. Linked to this is a belief that share ownership is good in itself. Increasing the proportion of the population which owns shares is seen to lead to a greater understanding of the importance of wealth creation, which in turn is seen to lead to greater entrepreneurial activity in general. Market forces are seen as the driving force in society, such that the economy will be strong when government is able to leave the private sector alone to generate wealth. Long-term future prosperity is seen as directly related to privatization.

It would be foolish to deny that privatization has brought benefits, and not only to the already affluent. Some nationalized industries were extremely inefficient and badly organized. They responded slowly, if at all, to consumer demands. Some were overstaffed, and had more than their fair share of workers who avoided the work they were paid to do, recognizing that their strong union position made it almost impossible for them to be sacked.

In the same way, some local authorities were excessively bureaucratic and slow-moving. In the worst areas, repairs to council houses were a very long time coming and then done badly. Echoing Henry Ford, the choice of door colour was either blue or blue. The main benefit enjoyed by such tenants was heavily subsidized non-means-tested rents, which sometimes was a subsidy from the poor to the reasonably well-off.

Yet, as will be discussed in more detail later, there are costs to be paid for the perceived benefits of privatization. While bad examples of public provision could be found, there were also councils offering high-quality housing services, and nationalized industries which were efficient and gave good service to customers. One of the major dangers of privatization of welfare services is simply that it may be a euphemism for a cut in services, and in all the different forms of privatization the net result is often an increase in inequality – the gains being achieved by a comparatively small number of those already wealthy, and the losses being directed to those already poor. Those who are old or unemployed, single-parent families, members of ethnic minority groups, low-paid manual workers, or women are likely to be forced to pay for the increased affluence of the rich.

Furthermore, the logic of such a broad ideology is that the degree of privatization that has occurred until now is merely a start. Peter Clark (1987), one of the proponents of further privatization, argues that 'The remaining size of the public sector defines the opportunities for privatization.' In other words, all public services have the potential for privatization. There have already been plans put forward by various groups for private prisons, the privatization of various government departments, and even the privatization of local authorities. Conceivably, the police, law courts, and armed forces could also be privatized. These, however, are still a long way in the future. The education service is a major area of government expenditure where the privatization process has already begun and is likely to accelerate rapidly.

Privatization in education

One of the first commentators to document the growth of privatization in education was Richard Pring. In this early paper for the pressure group Right to Comprehensive Education (1983), and in his later revised book chapter (1986), he describes the many separate, yet interlinked, ways in which the government is supporting and encouraging private education and gradually decreasing its support for the maintained sector. Within education, privatization is taking many different forms, many of which are similar to those occurring in other public social services. For example, within the maintained sector there has been increased charging for services, contracting out of elements of the service, and lack of adequate investment. Meanwhile, the government is encouraging alternative institutions, providing ideological and financial support for private education, and encouraging exit from state institutions. This chapter deals mainly within the process of privatization that occurred during the first two terms of the Conservative government since 1979. The more recent and obvious changes that are linked with the Education Reform Act of 1988 are discussed in the next chapter.

The Assisted Places Scheme

The most obvious example of the Conservative government's early active support for the private sector, both financially and ideologically, was the Assisted Places Scheme, which was introduced following the 1979 election victory. This scheme, designed to transfer high-ability pupils from the maintained sector to selected private schools, was the only aspect of the multi-faceted 1980 Education Act for which new expenditure was allowed. At that point it was envisaged that the total cost would be about £55 million each year in England and Wales, providing about 12,000 new places each year. That such new finance should have been made available at the very time when cuts were being made in the maintained sector ensured that the scheme met with hostility – some even from within the ranks of the Conservative Party itself. Pressures on the government eventually meant that the size of the scheme had to be reduced, so that the financial allocation for 1985/86 was set at £34 million, with a total of 21,400 pupils holding assisted places (Tapper and Salter, 1986; Fitz *et al.*, 1986).

According to the government information leaflets, the scheme in England and Wales was set up to 'give able children a wider range of educational opportunity' by giving 'help with tuition fees at independent schools to parents who could not otherwise afford them' (DES, 1985). (The scheme for Scotland has several major differences, see Walford, 1988a.) The assisted places are thus means-tested. Selection criteria are decided by the individual schools, but are usually based on academic promise and performance. A selected child whose parents have an income of under £7,259 (in 1988/9) receives a free place. Those parents with an income of £10,000 contribute £402, whilst those with £15,000 contribute £1,647 per annum.

Table 9 Number of assisted places accepted in 1987, including places not previously taken up

	11+		*12+*		*13+*		*16+*	
			Number of places available					
	3,925		173		439		1,011	
			Number of places accepted					
	M	P	M	P	M	P	M	P
Girls	1,160	423	47	43	71	78	208	225
	1,517	429	40	24	128	204	127	181
Total	2,677	852	87	67	199	282	335	406

Note. M maintained, P private school.
Source. Assisted Places Committee questionnaire of 229 out of 233 participating schools.

Table 9 shows how the number of pupils with assisted places in October 1987 according to whether they previously attended a maintained or a private school. One of the requirements of the scheme is that 60 per cent of places should be offered to pupils who were previously in state-maintained schools, but it can be seen from table 9 that, whether by choice or lack of other candidates, this proportion has been met only for the 11 + intake. At all other levels the number of pupils from the private sector is higher than 40 per cent. Overall, however, the far greater number of entrants at 11+ means that the total proportion does meet the 60 per cent criterion. The schools have also attempted to ensure that pupils with parents with the lowest possible income receive the assisted places. This is the obvious thing for a school to do, especially where the schools has its own means-tested scholarship scheme.

It is not the purpose of this chapter to try to evaluate the success of the scheme in its own terms against the objectives set for it by government. An ESRC-funded study of the scheme has already looked into these matters (see Edwards *et al.*, 1989; Whitty and Edwards, 1984; Fitz *et al.*, 1986). The authors show that, in their local case studies, about a third of pupils on the scheme came from single-parent families and 25 per cent of the siblings of their sample pupils were, or had recently been, at private schools. While their evidence supports the claim that the majority of the places are held by children from families with low or 'modest' incomes, they also point to a low participation rate by manual working-class families. The authors suggest that 'a considerable proportion of assisted place holders come from submerged middle class backgrounds already well endowed with cultural capital' (Fitz *et al.*, 1986: 185). These results are in broad agreement with those from a small-scale study by Douse (1985).

I have argued elsewhere (Walford, 1987a) that, although the schools might wish to present their participation in the scheme as largely altruistic, for some of them the Assisted Places Scheme is now vital to their continued health and success. Several of the schools now have a very high proportion of their pupils on APS, with over fifty schools having 30-40 per cent. A further forty four schools have more than 40 per cent, and the average APS schools had 118 pupils in the scheme. Government funding, at a far higher cost per pupil than within the maintained sector, thus directly supports private provision. An article by Richard Wilkinson, headmaster of King Edward's School, Witley, makes the importance of APS support clear.

> It will not therefore surprise the reader if I defend the APS. I believe that it is a good scheme. But I must be honest. It is a good scheme partly because it helps independent schools. I reject the tendentious arguments of Tory politicians that the APS helps children as opposed to schools. It does both. While a very small minority of schools on the scheme – the Winchesters and the Sedberghs – may indeed have no *need* of state support, the majority will have benefited considerably . . . Many schools will be 'sick' if the APS is withdrawn – sick financially and in terms of the loss of children of ability.
>
> [Wilkinson, 1986: 59]

The benefits of which Wilkinson writes are not just financial. The APS gives schools a better chance of being the sort of schools which they wish to be. For example, over the last decade or more there has been a steady decline in the number of boarders, and this has presented particular problems for schools in isolated areas. Even boarding schools in large towns would often prefer to maintain their 'boarding school ethos' if they can, for it is is generally recognized that to have too large a proportion of day pupils severely impairs the 'full-time, total' institutional aspects of boarding schools. The APS does not provide boarding fees, but each year places are made available to pupils who board. The difference between the two fees is provided from the schools' own funds, from friends, relations, or even the parents themselves from wealth rather than from income (Walford, 1987a). In 1987, 1,677 APS pupils were boarders – 6.2 per cent of the total.

At a more fundamental level, the APS also allows the schools to maintain high academic entry standards. By selecting APS pupils of high ability, schools are able to maintain numbers without having to take in additional fee-payers who might have lower academic ability. In their report on their local case studies Fitz *et al.* (1986: 190) state:

> there certainly were independent schools in our sample which were keen to recruit well-motivated assisted place pupils rather than the new market constituency which the less prestigious schools were being forced to appeal to in the absence of LEA place holders in a situation of falling rolls.

In a similar vein, Clive Griggs (1985:91) argues, slightly more colourfully, that the APS acted as a lifeline for some of the lesser known private schools, and states, 'by boosting the intake of highly academically able children, one head confessed to me that it had prevented his small schools sliding down the "Gin and Jaguar" belt of the minor public schools'.

The presence of APS pupils can also be shown to have had the effect of increasing the academic honours that the private schools can claim. In 1987, 56 per cent of the assisted place sixth-form leavers (N = 1,345) went on to university and a total of 76 per cent went on to higher education. Given the select nature of the students, these figures might actually seem rather low, but they are higher than for the private sector as a whole. Within the HMC schools, in 1987, 46 per cent of post-O/A level leavers went on to university and 62 per cent went on to higher education, whilst for GSA schools the figures were 31 per cent and 46 per cent. The assisted place students thus increase the higher education entry rates of the schools, and thus artificially widen further the differences between maintained and private schools in their success rates. Given that the APS pupils are strictly selected, mainly on their academic ability, it comes as no surprise that they do well, and we saw in chapter three that this success may have nothing to do with the schools at all.

But every highly academically able child transferred to the private sector is potentially one more 'success', such that the scheme gives the illusion that the differences between the two sectors are greater than they really are.

This last point is linked with the final, and perhaps most important, way in which the private schools derive support from government through the APS, which is the degree of ideological support for private schools which it exemplifies. According to Mark Carlisle, then Secretary of State at the DES, the aim of the Assisted Places Scheme was '. . . to give certain children a greater opportunity to pursue a particular form of academic education that was regrettably not otherwise, particularly in cities, available to them' (quoted in Griggs, 1985: 89). The implication of the scheme was clearly that the private sector was 'better' than the maintained sector and that the maintained sector, especially in cities, was of insufficient quality to ensure academic success. As access to professional and middle-class occupations is now largely dependent on academic credentials, the message was that the government and DES had little confidence that its own schools were the appropriate place for aspiring middle-class parents to send their children. There implications were immediately evident to the Society of Education Officers, who questioned the educational basis of the scheme (SEO, 1979), and to John Rae, then headmaster of Westminster School, who felt that:

> The Scheme was based on a false premise: that an independent school was automatically a better place to educate a bright child. But in some parts of the country, the maintained schools were perfectly capable of enabling a bright child to fulfil his potential. To help parents move a child in those circumstances would be a waste of public money and an insult to the maintained sector.
>
> [Rae, 1981: 179]

Technically, Rae was incorrect, for the scheme does not automatically assume that *all* independent schools are 'better' than maintained ones; about 250 of the schools that initially applied to be part of the scheme were rejected because their academic or other standards were considered indequate. (These schools were thus presumably 'worse' than maintained schools – a judgement that was very unlikely to be given prominence in any literature to prospective parents.) In practice, however, Rae is correct, for the introduction of APS has raised the status of all private sector schools. The message behind the scheme is that the government recommends that parents with children of high academic ability should make every effort to move those children out of the maintained sector into the private sector, for the government itself believes that the private sector is superior. This belief is reflected at a personal level by the fact that the vast majority of members of the Conservative Cabinet have chosen to send their children to private rather than maintained schools (Rawnsley, 1986).

The APS was thus a key element in the government's privatization strategy for education, and in many ways can be seen as similar to selling off council houses at a discount. The costs to the government per pupil were higher than in the maintained sector, but such a price was seen as worth paying to emphasize the supposed superiority of the private service. The scheme also had the effect of blurring the boundaries between the two systems and making it appear that parents were able to choose what form of educational provision they wished for their children. Schooling thus took a step towards becoming just another consumer product, where parents were customers choosing between different suppliers on the basis of needs and desires. The further 'blurring of the boundaries' was also to be a key element of the 1988 Education Reform Act, which is discussed in the next chapter.

Government funding through charitable status

Since 1979 the Conservative government has made numerous attempts to encourage charitable giving. Welfare and social service-related charities have been encouraged, and substantial amounts of government money have been directed through various charities rather than through government departments. Such measures are consistent with the government's general policy of favouring private provision, and should be seen as part of the overall privatization process. In the present context, the importance of these changes is that the majority of the major private schools are educational charities and thus benefit from any new concessions made to charities by government. Indeed, the government's ideological commitment to private education may be seen as one of the contributory factors behind many of the taxation changes that have been made since 1979.

As charities the schools qualify for a considerable and diverse range of tax concessions, including rate relief and exemptions from corporation tax, income tax, and capital gains tax. Moreover, there are tax exemptions for donors to charities and for transfers to charities, while charitable trusts are exempt from inheritance tax. They are also exempt from stamp duty for instruments effecting conveyances, transfers, or leases. The private schools are also outside the VAT system, an advantage which is not related to charitable status, but which is probably far more important to them than all the other privileges (Robson and Walford, 1989).

In the first few years after 1979 the government made numerous changes in taxation to encourage charitable giving. For example, the government quickly reduced the period necessary for charitable covenants to attract tax relief from 'over six' to 'over three' years in order to encourage a flow of funds from private sources to the voluntary sector. It further introduced relief from higher rates of taxation for covenanted payments up to a maximum of £3,000 per year. This was increased to £5,000 in 1983 and to £10,000 in 1985. At that point individual relief from high rates of tax for individuals covenanting payments was of particular importance to private schools. While parents were never able to obtain tax relief for school fees for their own children in this way, relations and friends could do so instead. Grandparents, in particular, often wished to support the private education of their grandchildren, and there was a gain to be made by covenanting to pay each year up to the child's personal allowance. While this was insufficient to pay the fees of most schools if the fee were required immediately, advance planning and the use of life assurance policies enabled a greater proportion of the fees to be paid in this way. The raising of the maximum amount for relief from higher rates of tax enabled high-earning grandparents or others to benefit from a covenant to more children. It is estimated that perhaps 20 per cent of pupils had received help from grandparents and others in this way in the mid-1980s (Robson and Walford, 1989). However, in 1988 the whole system was swept away in an attempt to simplify the tax system overall. New covenants of this sort no longer have any effect for tax purposes.

Early Conservative legislation also introduced exemption from stamp duty, capital transfer tax, and development land tax (now abolished) on gifts to charities, and gave tax relief for employers on the salary costs of employees seconded to charities. The last of these concessions was extended to maintained schools only in 1986, and is beginning to be used by schools to provide Industrial Fellows and the like who aim to generate greater links between schools and industry (Walford, 1988c). A further change concerns capital transfer tax, which was renamed inheritance tax in 1986. Until 1983 there was tax exemption on legacies to charities of up to £250,000. In the 1983 Budget, however, this limit was removed such that all gifts were exempt. This may appear to be a fairly minor change, for single legacies of over a quarter of a million pounds to any charity are rare. On these rare occasions, however, the change can be of major significance. For example, in July 1986 Norman Sharpe, OBE, a bachelor and old boy of Giggleswick School, died and left a million pounds to the school. The exact details are complicated and depend on individual circumstances, but had he died prior to 1983 that million could have been reduced by up to £450,000 in tax. By his living a few more years the school was able to receive the whole of the £1 million.

A further new type of tax relief was introduced in 1986. For the first time companies were able to claim tax relief on one-off gifts to charities up to a maximum of 3 per cent of the ordinary dividends paid by the company. Unsolicited gifts, benefactions, and highly organized appeals are now an important way by which private schools finance new buildings and facilities (Griggs, 1985: 66; Walford, 1986a: 212). Individual schools now launch appeals for at least a half a million pounds – some for much more. Such appeals are very carefully organized, and are not aimed primarily at the parents of boys or girls at present in the school. Instead, they aim to get a small number of large donations from major companies, institutions, and individuals which can then be supplemented by a host of smaller donations. Contacts with old boys and girls who have sometimes risen in their career to a very senior position are thus vital, for its is the director of major companies who are able to ensure that their own schools can receive a share of the company's regular charitable contributions.

The importance of this particular tax change is that companies are often reluctant to covenant donations for a period of as long as four years, for the instability of the present economic climate makes predictions of future profit margins very difficult. The introduction of tax relief on single donations by companies is likely to help schools considerably in attracting financial support from companies for specific one-off appeals. Schools will be able to benefit from end-of-tax-year windfall profits, or simply obtain a share of any sudden generosity on the part of companies.

Although the changes in the structure of taxation in favour of charities have been many, it is difficult to assess their overall effect, for, while the structure of taxation has been changed to encourage charitable giving, the rates of taxation have progressively fallen as part of the government's general policy of reducing the 'burden of taxation'. The concessions given to charities become less significant as tax rates fall, and indeed many of the changes in structure may be seen as an attempt to compensate for losses which charities would otherwise suffer as a consequence of declining tax rates.

In addition, the 1988 Budget appeared to mark a general change in policy towards government support for charities. Tax rates were once again reduced, but there was little in terms of compensation through changes in the structure. Concern about misuse of charitable status (Woodfield, 1987) and the growing use of charities for tax avoidance (Tutt, 1985) appears to have led to a change in general policy. Further government financial assistance to the private schools can thus be expected to be through specific directed policies, and the increase in APS announced within a short time of the 1988 Budget might be seen as an example of this occurring.

It must also be recognized that loss of charitable status would only add about 5 per cent to the costs of most private schools. The direct effect of removal of such status would cause major problems only for a small number of schools at the margins. But it may be that, as Salter and Tapper (1985) argue, the symbolic and ideological aspects of charitable status are of more importance to the system as a whole than the direct financial gains.

Other government funding and support

In chapter two we saw that the government has given continued direct and indirect support to private schools since 1833. This support has taken many different and changing forms over the years, some of which have been highly controversial and some of which have gone largely unquestioned. It is not possible or desirable to catalogue the many other ways in which support for private schools is currently channelled. This has been done elsewhere (Griggs, 1985; Labour Party, 1980). Nevertheless it is worth noting some of the other ways in which the privatization process is proceeding through growing support for the private schools.

Table 10 Pupils in ISIS schools receiving contributions to fees

Year	From LEA	APS	From school	Other sources	HM forces
1982	19,904	4,679	30,902	7,529	10,416
1983	16,930	9,769	35,544	7,364	13,705
1984	12,873	14,324	39,321	6,227	14,089
1985	10,492	20,023	40,785	5,585	15,016
1986	9,763	22,943	42,989	4,644	15,064
1987	8,512	25,935	43,991	5,111	15,768
1988	8,096	28,381	57,148	4,994	16,287

Source. ISIS Annual Census.

Table 10, for example, indicates some interesting changes in number of pupils receiving assistance with fees. The data are drawn from annual ISIS surveys and are not strictly comparable year to year, owing to slight changes in the number of schools involved. However, the general picture is a reliable one. As might be expected at a time when the LEAs are hard pressed for finance, and when the new Assisted Places Scheme was growing, the number of pupils supported by LEAs is reducing. It is worth noting that the rate of reduction in LEA support is less than the rate of growth in APS support. The increase in the number of pupils being helped directly by the schools themselves is probably related to the APS increase. By ensuring that, of those whom the school wishes to help, the pupils with the poorest parents are given assisted places, the school is able to help a larger number of other parents from the same amount of scholarship money, by giving less to each.

The final column of the table indicates that the number of pupils with parents in the armed forces and attending private schools has increased dramatically. The government pays boarding school allowances for the boarding education of military personnel, irrespective of whether they are stationed overseas or not, on the grounds that continuity of education is important and that military families are faced with frequent and unpredictable moves. The Ministry of Defence pays some two-thirds of the average fees of a representative group of schools. The most important reason for the increase here is the decrease in the boarding places available in the maintained sector. Largely owing to government cuts in local authority funding, rather than any lack of demand or need, LEAs have been forced to close many of their boarding schools. In 1978 there were 103 state schools offering 10,109 boarding places, but by 1987 there were only 71, with 6,100 places (O'Connor, 1986). These schools were previously heavily used by military personnel, who have thus been forced to seek boarding within the private sector instead. The effect of the general reduction in maintained boarding also changes the 'image' of the remaining maintained schools, such that a higher proportion of the children are likely to have clearly defined 'boarding needs'. This may make the remaining schools less desirable for HM forces parents and thus add to the increase in private boarding.

Although much of the discussion about government subsidy of places in private schools is now in terms of the Assisted Places Scheme, it is worth noting that there is also another scheme, the Aided Places Scheme, which started in 1981 and provides assistance with fees for pupils attending five specialist music and ballet schools in England and one music school in Scotland. These six include Chetham's School of Music, the Royal Ballet School and Wells Cathedral School. The assistance provided under this scheme is means-tested, but on a far more generous scale than that for the Assisted Places Scheme. Also, in contrast to the Assisted Places Scheme, assistance is available for the boarding element as well as for tuition, and for children below the age of 11 in some cases. In 1985/6 the total cost of the scheme for the five English schools was £2.9 million for 446 pupils, equivalent to over £6,400 per pupil.

Privatization within the maintained sector

The government's increased support for the private sector is only part of the process of privatization that is gradually occurring, for rather different aspects of the privatization process are taking place in the maintained sector. The 1944 Education Act embodied the idea that secondary education should be available to all children according to age, ability, and aptitude rather than according to parental ability or willingness to pay. While there have been continued debates about how provision should be made available according to ability and aptitude, until recently it has gone almost unquestioned that educational provision within the maintained sector should not depend on parental finance. In the last few years, however, this assumption has been challenged, and very many maintained schools have found themselves dependent upon private resources to supplement the funding obtained from the local education authority. Richard Pring (1986) carefully charts the way in which services that should be free within the maintained sector have become increasingly dependent upon private means. He discusses the many ways in which parents or pupils in maintained schools now pay for what were previously regarded as essentials of schooling. Parents not only pay for pencils, art materials, books, and paper but in places, through covenants, help pay the wages of laboratory assistants, schools secretaries, and the general running costs of the schools. In some cases parental contributions exceed the amount provided for running costs by the local education authority. Parents at Budmouth School, Weymouth, raised more than £25,000 in four years through covenants, a school in Somerset raised £60,000 in the same time (Kirkman, 1987). According to Neil Kinnock (1986: 139), parents contribute an estimated £40 million per year to the costs of *essential* teaching and learning materials. This extra money is spread throughout the system in an inegalitarian way, such that a report by Hertfordshire County Council in 1987 showed that its most fortunate secondary schools had thirty-seven times as much additional income as the most deprived (Judd, 1987). This increased privatization of the maintained sector has the double effect of increasing the differences between individual state maintained schools, and also of lessening the psychological difference for parents between paying for education at a fee-paying school and paying for it in a maintained school. It might be argued that this process is very similar to that occurring in the National Health Service, where the level of government funding is insufficient to meet growing needs.

The government's deliberate policy of restricting resources available for state education, at a time of falling school rolls (which necessitate greater funding per pupil), and at a time when the price of books and scientific and technical equipment has risen far faster than the general rate of inflation, has been of direct benefit to the private sector. Various HMI reports, with their accounts of schools with leaking roofs, broken windows, and a poor state of decoration and repair of buildings, have made it clear that state maintained schools are seriously underfunded (DES, 1986a) Inevitably, there are growing differences between schools in the facilities that are available, with schools in poorer areas falling rapidly behind. This gap in the quality of what is available is very evident in the quality of repair and decoration of the school buildings themselves. Maintenance has frequently been seen as an easy target for short-term savings. It has become common for LEAs to supply paint and decorating materials, but rely on voluntary parent or teacher labour to do the actual work. Payment for services in this case is thus not in direct financial term, but in the form of free labour. Again, there is a wide range in the ability of schools to recruit such volunteer labour from their parents.

This neglect of the bricks and mortar is just one part of the general neglect of the system. Sir Keith Joseph's disastrous handling of the long 1985-6 dispute with the teachers could hardly have been organized better to help the private sector. Throughout his period of office at the Department of Education and Science, Sir Keith appeared to take every opportunity possible to emphasize his belief that the quality of teaching in the maintained sector was poor. His emphasis on 'raising standards', 'increased relevance', 'greater accountability', and 'assessment of teachers' all implied that teachers in the maintained sector were not doing their job properly. With hardly ever a word of praise for teachers among constant criticism, Sir Keith had ensured that teacher morale was at a very low ebb even before the 1985-6 dispute. The dispute itself brought considerable disruption to classes, and practically all extra-curricular activity ceased.

This clear criticism of the maintained sector, and implied preference for the private, have been sustained by Kenneth Baker since he became Secretary of State for Education and Science. Teachers have had a pay and changed working conditions settlement imposed upon them and their negotiating rights removed. Such actions are unlikely to raise morale.

There are several other changes within the maintained sector which can be seen as part of this privatization process. For example, there is an increase in the contraction out of cleaning and school meals services. Where both these services had previously been provided directly by the LEA, they are now offered for tender to the most 'efficient' private bidder. Manual staff transferring to new privatized contracts have often found that the increased 'efficiency' has been achieved through reduced pay and poorer working conditions. Another aspect is the increased renting out of schools buildings for profit rather than according to the intrinsic worth of the activity taking place. The school itself and those needy groups in the community have sometimes been squeezed out and replaced by profit-making lettings. There is even a direct analogy between what is occurring in schools and the sale of nationalized companies and assets, for in 1981 the amount of land deemed necessary for sports, playing fields, and leisure for each school was reduced. 'Surplus' land has thus been sold off for building and other uses, for a once-only profit. Sales of redundant schools buildings, caused by falling rolls, have been encouraged by government and the Audit Commission, even where these sales involve new buildings which might be of considerable use to the community, and where they could have reverted to school use when schools rolls begin to rise again.

Pring (1987) outlines a whole new area of privatization in schools with the change in funding for in-service training for teachers in 1987. Money has been shifted from a national pool (which could be used only for designated courses) to the LEAs, so that they can plan and provide local in-service either internally or by purchasing the services of universities, colleges, or private consultants. The introduction of 'Baker days' has also led to in-service work becoming more schools-based, and there has developed a whole new breed of private education consultants to help organize these in-service days. Retired head teachers, higher education academics, psychologists, and the like are now conducting school-based training on a privatized profit-making basis.

Education as a consumer product

At the start of this chapter it was argued that privatization can take many very different forms, and that it acts as a 'general approach which can generate and focus policy ideas'. At the very basic ideological level it is linked with a belief in the 'natural' goodness of the market place and the benefits of competition between suppliers. In terms of the privatization of education, this means that as the process has progressed schooling has come to be thought of more and more as an individual consumer product. Good parents are those who 'shop around' for the best that is on offer, whether it be in the private or in the maintained sector. In this very general sense, the government's policies of giving greater freedom of choice to parents using the maintained sector can be seen as part of the process of privatization.

Some degree of choice of schools is, of course, highly desirable. For planning, it is usual to assume that most parents are likely to wish to send their children to the nearest or most convenient school, so it makes sense to draw rough catchment areas around each school to guide this process. But some parents may not wish to use the nearest school, so, where it is possible, it is reasonable that they should be allowed to use the school of their choice. Section 76 of the 1944 Education Act stated that 'so far as is compatible with the provision of efficient instruction and training and the avoidance of unreasonable public expenditure, pupils are to be educated in accordance with the wishes of their parents'. Stillman and Maychell (1986) explain that this section was originally intended to give Roman Catholics and Anglicans a choice of the *type* of schools they could use, but fairly quickly it was interpreted to mean that parents should be given a choice between individual schools. Usually children were allocated to a school and then their parents were allowed to appeal against the allocation. Prior to 1980, LEAs usually kept this right of appeal rather quiet in order to simplify their planning and to avoid problems of oversubscribed schools. With a limited stock of schools

79

and rooms in schools, not everyone could have a free choice, but those parents who pushed hard enough usually got their way, and the vast majority of children attended the school to which they were allocated.

Parental voices began to be heard in the 1970s, and by the end of the decade both the major political parties were planning changes to give parents greater choice. The main problem was that falling rolls had led many LEAs to try to keep schools open by balancing the numbers of pupils between schools. Parents found that the LEA would not allow them to use the school of their choice even though there was clearly room in the school buildings for extra children. The number of individual appeals to the Secretary of State for Education and Science was causing an administrative nightmare.

Clearly, though, the idea of increasing choice between schools for parents was attractive to the Conservative government. It was believed that increased choice would stimulate competition between schools, and thus raise the quality and nature of what was on offer to meet the demands of parents. It is interesting that pupil choice was never considered! The 1980 Education Act thus included major sections on parental choice, including the idea that LEAs should publish the *intended* intake numbers for each school, and make the right of choice clear to parents. Appeal committees were also set up, and schools were required to publish a considerable amount of information about themselves so that parents could make a more informed choice. The 1980 Act did not have quite the practical impact that was intended, as LEAs were still able to fix the intake numbers in an arbitrary way, but it was a further step in changing the way in which schools have become viewed. It emphasized the individual consumer making choices between providers of services, and thus de-emphasized any larger social functions that schools might be thought to have. Schooling was increasingly seen as for the individual's good. It was only for the good of society in so far as that coincided with the good of the individual.

This product/consumer model of schooling has gradually permeated most schools, and is evident in the general orientation of many of the staff and in the language that is used to talk about schools and the curriculum. Schools now have a 'senior management team', often with clear 'line management'. A curriculum is now 'delivered' or 'implemented'; the school is concerned with its 'public relations' and its 'image'; children become 'inputs' and examination successes 'outputs'; 'consumer research' is conducted and 'new markets' are sought. The language and mode of operation of industry has come to be accepted within schools, such that the next steps in the process of privatization become easier to take.

Privatization in higher education

Although the main concern of this book is with private schools and the privatization of the school sector, it is worth briefly considering the similar processes that are occurring within the full range of educuational provision. As indicated in chapter one, there is now extensive private provision at both the pre- and post-school levels. The provision of post-school education and training on a profit-making basis, in particular, has grown dramatically, but there are no comprehensive figures available. Griggs (1985: 111–14) describes the range from secretarial schools to crammers for pre-university students who fail to obtain sufficiently high A-level grades for their desired course. Oxford alone has some twenty separate tutorial colleges, often taking the failures from the private schools. One guide to private further education lists about 600 different colleges and related establishments. Language schools are also an expanding area of operation and range from the highly proficient and well established to the dubious and temporary.

These areas of post-school provision have, of course, existed for decades, and their recent growth has as much to do with the increasing importance of qualifications and credentials as with the government's direct policies on privatization. The government's part here has been in encouraging the change of climate such that private provision has become not only acceptable but, for many, preferable.

Although it has largely gone unrecognized, a similar process of privatization is occurring in higher education. Perhaps one of the reasons for the lack of recognition is that the existing private sector of higher education is very small – there being only one independent British university, the University of Buckingham. However, a brief study of the development of that institution clearly indicates the government's support for the private sector in higher education (Walford, 1988b).

The proposal to establish a private, non-state-supported institution of higher education was first put forward in 1967, and the University College of Buckingham was officially opened by Margaret Thatcher in 1976. On her election in 1979, Mrs Thatcher quickly showed her support for private higher education by ensuring that students at the college became eligible for local authority mandatory grants. A greater show of support occurred in March 1983 when a royal charter was granted to the college, so that it could award its own degrees and could restyle itself as the University of Buckingham. (For details, see Shaw and Blaug, 1988.) At this point the college had only about 500 students, who were studying a limited range of academic subjects, with facilities which few would consider to be up to university standards. Yet, while a charter was granted to Buckingham, the polytechnics, with long and distinguished pedigrees, years of experience, and far superior facilities, were denied the privilege.

The government's direct support for private higher education was also clearly indicated in 1985 on the publication, by the right-wing Institute of Economic Affairs (IEA), of a radical proposal for the privatization of British business schools, written by two professors at City University Business School (Griffiths and Murray, 1985). Although it is a relatively small organization, the various publications of the IEA have recently had a major influence in setting the tone of debate in education on such questions as parental choice, vouchers, and student loans, and the ideas put forward on business schools were treated with considerable respect by the government. Briefly, the proposal was that postgraduate business education should be removed from existing universities and gathered together in distinct business schools and that, over a three-year period, all postgraduate business school activity should cease to be government-funded and should be funded by fees and endowments instead. The Secretary of State for Education and Science caused a copy of the report to be sent to universities teaching business and management studies with a covering letter from his department which stated:

> In inviting comment on the Paper the Secretary of State wishes to hear views, not only on reforms proposed by Professor Griffiths and Professor Murray but also on the criticisms of existing provision and on the suggested cause of the weaknesses which they detect. The Secretary of State is himself sympathetic to many of the ideas expressed in the paper and with the proposition that business schools should rely wholly, or to a much larger extent than at present, on income from private sources.

Partly as a result of these proposals, the Secretary of State also called an informal meeting with a small number of vice-chancellors at which the possibility of privatizing whole universities was discussed. The idea was that a few universities might be given a large once-only endowment by the government and would thereafter receive no further public money through the University Grants Committee. In the event, neither of these ideas came to fruition. The amount of endowment required by individual universities to opt out was seen as too large for the government to contemplate, and the only slight change to management education was that both Manchester and London Business Schools did rather badly in the 1986 allocations made by the UGC. Both these initiatives, however, indicate the strength of feeling towards privatization, competition, and finding alternatives to government funding for higher education. The privatization idea was revitalized in September 1988, when Sir Graham Hills, Vice-chancellor of Strathclyde University, suggested an experimental 'state entitlements' or voucher scheme for about ten universities and polytechnics. The idea was that these institutions should be allowed to charge full fees and be funded by them rather than by a block grant from government. It was seen as having the advantage that students could then be sponsored by bursaries and could add to their 'voucher' if the fees were set higher. Kenneth Baker welcomed the proposal a few days later in a speech to the Committee of Vice-chancellors and Principals, as he saw it as part of a plan to increase the number of students in higher education without incurring extra government cost.

In spite of this very clear direct support for privatization, there has generally been a reluctance to conceptualize recent changes in higher education in these terms. Perhaps one of the reasons for this reluctance is that, formally and legally, universities are *already* private non-profit-making institutions. It is only in the last few decades that the universities have become so dependent upon direct government funding – before that, they were much more clearly private institutions competing 'in the market place'. However, by and large, universities no longer regard themselves as private institutions but as part of the public education system. In a way, the present changes must thus be regarded as a 're-privatization' in terms of attitudes as much as funding, as the government wishes them to become more entrepreneurial and competitive, to be more diverse, and to provide a variety of services to customers.

In order to promote these changes the government has, especially since 1981, gradually reduced public expenditure on universities. As shown in detail elsewhere (Walford, 1987d, 1988b), there has been a swift cut-back in government funding overall, and universities have been encouraged to seek alternative sources of funding. In particular, they have been urged to go to industry and commerce to make up the short-fall, either by offering specific research or services to companies, or by relying on the altruistic generosity of firms to support professorial chairs and donate money for buildings and facilities. Some universities have been spectacularly successful in attracting such funding, but there are still unanswered questions about the extent to which such support is either desirable or possible to sustain in the long term.

More usually, faced with falling income, individual universities have been forced to become more 'efficient', which has meant widespread closure and merger of departments and faculties and a decline in the academic work force of more than 8 per cent in the four years from 1981. This decrease was achieved by way of massive early retirement and 'golden handshake' programmes, aimed especially at those members of staff on tenured contracts. The limited number of new appointments which are now being made are usually on short-term contracts, such that universities gain increased 'flexibility' in the management of their work force.

The Education Reform Act of 1988 takes this process of re-privatization of the universities several stages further, with the introduction of contract funding through a new University Funding Council, and the abolition of tenure for all new appointments. At the same time the polytechnics and major colleges of higher education have been removed from local education authority control to become a new group of independent entrepreneurial higher education institutions, funded by a new Polytechnics and colleges Funding Council on a similar contract basis. All this, however, is the subject of the next chapter, where the Education Reform Act with its many overt privatization policies is discussed.

Summary

Privatization is a broad process which takes a number of different forms. This chapter has shown that the process of privatization that has occurred in the social and welfare services has many similarities with the current process of change in education.

The chapter examines the present government's financial and ideological support for private schooling, looking in particular at the Assisted Places Scheme and the support which schools gain by virtue of their charitable status. It also outlines some of the privatization processes within the maintained sector, which have the effect of blurring the boundaries between the private and maintained sectors. Finally, it is shown that privatization is also a major strategy within higher education.

Chapter five

The 1988 Education Reform Act

The Conservative Party's 1987 general election manifesto put forward radical proposals for change within education. At the school level, the changes were outlined in terms of 'four major reforms'. First, a national curriculum was to be established, with attainment levels and associated testing of performance at around 7, 11, 14, and 16. Second, governing bodies of all secondary schools and many primary schools were to be given control over their own budgets. Third, parental choice was to be increased by ensuring that numbers in maintained schools could not be artificially restricted and by establishing a pilot network of city technology colleges. Within this area of reform was a pledge to continue to defend the right to private education and a plan to expand the Assisted Places Scheme. Fourth, state schools were to be given the right to opt out of local education authority control and become directly funded by the DES instead.

Any of these four areas would present a major challenge to the nature and administrative structure of the existing system of state maintained schools. All four together were designed to bring about a revolution, and this is indeed what has occurred as a result of the 1988 Education Act. In this chapter it will be shown that while two of the four reforms can immediately be seen as central to the privatization strategy, all four are actually part of the same overall strategy. This does not mean that all the changes made in the Education Act can be as the direct result of an ideological commitment to privatization. For example, the strong attack on local education authorities is not only due to a desire for privatization, but can be also seen as the result of some of the Labour-controlled councils taking a firm stand on the implementation of the anti-racist and anti-sexist policies. Some LEAs had also attempted to implement anti-heterosexist initiatives which, in the moral panic surrounding AIDS, had provoked some extreme reactions. The Education Reform Act also has a strong tendency towards greater central control of education, for the Secretary of State has been given very many new powers under the Act. However, a desire to continue with the

85

privatization process is the most important single strand which draws together what otherwise appears to be a disparate range of educational changes.

One of the remarkable aspects of the Education Reform Act is that such a major piece of legislation should be in force little more than a year after the election manifesto promises were made. The Conservative Party manifesto was published in May 1987, and Margaret Thatcher was elected to serve a third term in June 1987. A series of so-called consultation papers were issued during the summer of 1987, including one on the national curriculum, one on financial delegation to schools, another on grant maintained schools, and yet another on admission limits in maintained schools.

All these were issued in July, with comments required by September. Very little time was thus given for any real consultation on these important proposals, and even less time was given for reading and accommodating to any responses and suggestions. The Education Reform Bill was presented to the House of Commons in November 1987, and had a speedy, though at times heated and controversial, passage through both Houses of Parliament, to become law in July 1988. The House of Lords, even with its in-built Conservative majority, had voted against several of the key issues, and some compromises had been made to the original proposals, but overall the Act remained very much as had been indicated in the consultation papers and as had been proposed in the Bill.

The Education Reform Act is a major piece of legislation. At the school level it deals with the ability of schools to charge for 'extras', open enrolment up to the physical limit of individual schools, local financial management of most schools, and changes in religious education. It establishes the national curriculum and associated testing, gives schools the right to opt out of LEA control, and puts city technology colleges on a legal footing. One major area where the parliamentary process did have an effect was with the changes proposed concerning the Inner London Education Authority. ILEA had been at the heart of many of the curriculum policies which had been attacked by the right. It also spent more per pupil than any other LEA. ILEA was solidly held by Labour and, unable to change this by democratic means, the Bill aimed at gradually dismembering ILEA by allowing individual councils to opt out of ILEA if they wished. As the Bill passed through Parliament, pressure grew to simplify the procedure by abolishing ILEA outright and devolving responsibility for education to the individual councils, and this is what was contained in the Act.

The Act also included very important changes to the structure and government of higher education, most of which were essential parts of a privatization process for this sector. The polytechnics and major colleges were removed from LEA control and established as institutions funded by a new Polytechnic and Colleges Funding Council. The original aim was that the new body should give funding on a contract basis, such that colleges would compete to provide the best value for money. This was subject to some modification in the passage through Parliament, but the essence remains. The seventy-year-old University Grants Committee was also replaced by a University Funding Council, which was intended to introduce the same sort of competition within the university sector. In order to increase 'managerial flexibility' the Act also abolished tenure for all new university academics. Throughout the sections on higher education, as elsewhere in the Act, the implementation of a gradual privatization process is a key feature (Walford 1988b).

In this chapter the key new elements of the government's educational privatization programme will be outlined. This will be done mainly at the descriptive level, but will include some of the criticisms and supportive comments of others. The chapter concentrates mainly on the practical problems and benefits of implementation. Chapter six is devoted to my own criticism and analysis of the programme at the level of the principles behind it, and to suggestions as to ways to combat some of the negative features of the Act.

City technology colleges

City technology colleges represent the most obvious of the moves to support the privatization process in education. The Education Reform Act gives the Secretary of State for Education and Science the power to enter into agreements to establish new private schools, to be called City Technology Colleges, and to make payments to the colleges in support of the education provided. However, the original announcement had been made nearly two years before the Education Act became law, and by the time the Act became law one CTC was nearly ready to open its door to pupils.

On 7 October 1986 the Secretary of State for Education and Science, Kenneth Baker, announced the creation of a pilot network of twenty centrally funded city technology colleges. The announcement was made during the Conservative Party conference which preceded the 1987 general election, but it had been rumoured in Whitehall and in the press for some time before. The idea of establishing such colleges was not, in fact, Kenneth Baker's but was derived from Keith Joseph's period of office and, in particular, the ideas of Stuart Sexton, who, as educational adviser to Sir Keith, had pioneered the Assisted Places Scheme.

At the general level, the 1980s had gradually made the calls from the political right for greater selection and differentiation between schools more respectable. Support for growth of the private sector was part of a broader call for greater 'choice in education'. To take just one example, in an Institute of Economic Affairs publication, Dennison (1984) called for more grammar schools, an extension of the Assisted Places Scheme, and the establishment of new private schools. He recommended that new independent schools might be encouraged by the handing over of the premises of schools to be closed, or by the provision of capital grants. He also suggested the introduction of genuine subsidies to private schools which might cover salaries and some capital expenditure. In April 1985 the Centre for Policy Studies, the government's 'think tank', called for experiments in DES-funded schools, with the aim of breaking the comprehensive model which had become established in most LEAs. This idea then became linked with the continuing problem of trying to encourage more young people to study science, technology, and engineering, and there were calls for 100 directly funded technical schools to be set up throughout England and Wales. There was talk of Crown primary schools, to be run on a direct grant basis, an idea particularly favoured by Stuart Sexton, who has established a private technological primary school in Surrey.

From the government's point of view, the problem with all these ideas was that they would necessitate greater expenditure, which was not seen as desirable. It was shown in the last chapter that privatization of social and welfare services is often accompanied by a decrease in the level of government support. New technology is very expensive, and while government had supported several modest schemes to increase the computing power available in schools, such funding would have to be continual and increasing to keep up with rapid changes. The city technology college idea is based on the recognition that additional funding for technological areas in schools might be available from industry and commerce. In other private schools funding mostly came from parents in the form of fees, but the CTC ideal allowed private money to flow from commercial backers instead. Industry could 'sponsor' a school in a similar way to sponsoring sporting competitions or music festivals. In this case there might even be a direct return on the investment in terms of more and better qualified scientists and technologists wishing to enter industry.

The city technology college plan that was put forward by Kenneth Baker was that a pilot network of about twenty colleges would be established to cater for 11 to 18-year-olds. They would be independent schools, run by educational trusts with close links with industry, but directly government funded in line with *per capita* expenditure in the local education authority. They would charge no fees, but sponsors would be expected to cover the extra costs involved in providing a highly technological curriculum and would make substantial contributions to both capital and current expenditure. But, while the desire to increase technological education was the major feature of the plan, it was made clear even at the first announcement that CTCs were also about broadening the range of choice of schools, destroying the comprehensive system, and reducing the powers of the LEAs.

A glossy brochure was published by the Department of Education and Science a week after the speech (DES, 1986b) and was sent to about 2,000 leading industrial and commercial concerns asking them to support the new venture. It was intended that the colleges would be established in urban areas, including the 'disadvantaged' inner cities, and that the first CTCs should come into operation in 1988. They were to serve substantial catchment areas, which would be defined in such a way that places would only be offered to about one in five or six children from within the catchment area. The aim was to admit pupils spanning the full range of ability within each area. Selection was to be based on:

> general aptitude, for example, as reflected in their progress and achievement in primary school; on their readiness to take advantage of the type of education offered in CTCs; on their parents' commitment to full-time education or training up to the age of 18, to the distinctive characteristics of the CTC curriculum, and to the ethos of the CTC.
> [DES, 1986b.]

Attendance at a CTC is expected to make heavy demands on the pupils, for it is anticipated that the school day and the school year will be longer than the legal minimum required. Pupils will be expected to take part in work experience, field trips, and extra-curricular activities as well. The curriculum will be unusually directive, giving pupils little choice in the subjects they study, even in years 4 and 5, and will include a broad and balanced curriculum up to age 16. The curriculum will keep to the 'substance of the national curriculum'. Although they are private schools, they will not be allowed to charge fees.

One of the important aspects about the CTC idea is that the schools are to be independent of central or local control. They will be able to negotiate their own salary scales and the conditions of service of their teaching staff, and will be able to employ people without 'qualified teacher' status without the special authorization of the DES.

Reaction to the scheme was swift and predominantly hostile. As might have been predicted, condemnation was strong from the teacher unions and from the Association of Metropolitan Authorities (AMA, 1987), but among the critics of the plan have also been the Confederation of British Industry and the Industrial Society. The opposition of the Association of Metropolitan Authorities was of major significance, for the association covers the inner-city areas for which the CTCs were destined, and which were predominantly under Labour control.

The site of the first CTC was announced in February 1987. The site chosen was in the metropolitan borough of Solihull, in the West

Midlands, most of which is far from the sort of inner-city deprived area that Kenneth Baker had in mind when he launched the CTCs. Its advantages were that it was Conservative-controlled, that the Director of Education had tried unsuccessfully to reintroduce selection a few years earlier (Walford and Jones, 1986), and that it was near enough to Birmingham to include some 'real' inner city within its catchment area. Falling school rolls necessitated the closure of some of the secondary schools in the borough, and the council was prepared to lease the buildings of Kingshurst Secondary School to form the base for the new CTC. The main financial backing was from Hanson Trust, a multinational financial empire, which gave £1 million while the more local Lucas Industries gave more limited support.

Other sponsors for colleges slowly emerged. Dixons proposed to sponsor one but did not have a site; Harry Djanogly, the millionaire chairman of the Nottingham Manufacturing textile company, offered support for a college to be newly built in Nottingham; Sir Philip Harris of Harris Queensway pledged money for another in London. By the time of the election, four colleges had at least some financial backing, and three of them had sites.

Strangely, as time went on, the city technology college idea began to look a less important part of the privatization process. The Conservative election manifesto, the consultation papers, and the eventual Education Reform Bill promised to all schools much of what had been seen as unique to CTCs. As will be discussed later in this chapter, all secondary schools were to be given budgetary independence, and schools were being given the chance to opt out of LEA control if they so wished. Governing bodies were to contain more business people and industrialists, and the national curriculum will ensure that much more technology is taught. All schools are already free to attract gifts and sponsorship if they can, and all are able to forge links with local industries and businesses.

In September 1987 Kenneth Baker visited some 'magnet' schools in Washington and New York. These schools are usually neighbourhood high schools which have a special enrichment programme which acts as a 'magnet' and draws other pupils from nearby areas who wish to specialize in that particular area (Metz 1986; Cooper, 1987). There is a range of schools with different specialisms; some are for science and mathematics, but others can be for dance or art. Kenneth Baker came back with a new justification of the CTCs in terms of their 'magnet' status, which for a while filled the educational press. However, in the USA magnet schools had been introduced to aid racial desegregation. Bussing pupils had failed, so special facilities were put into inner-city black schools to tempt white children in. Some of the schools have met with considerable success, but in the USA magnet schools were designed to serve social and egalitarian purposes, while in Britain CTCs legitimized inequality of provision, competition, and selection.

The City Technology College Trust, which had been set up to look for sites and sponsors, and help in the establishment of new colleges, was facing an uphill task. Of 1,800 firms approached to sponsor colleges, only seven initially responded positively. All the major companies, including those heavily reliant on science, declined to support the idea. This includes ICI, IBM, Shell, BP, and many others. One of the few supporters was BAT Industries, formerly British American Tobacco, which led to considerable controversy. Many educationalists and medics thought it unacceptable that a new school should be financed by a tobacco giant.

At the practical level there are several good reasons why industry and commerce may have been reluctant to become involved. The most important of these is directly related to the success of earlier government initiatives on the area of science and technology in schools. The Technical and Vocational Education Initiative, announced in 1982 as a pilot scheme and extended to cover all schools (though at a much reduced proportional cost) in 1986, has led to a great involvement of business and industry in state maintained schools. There are secondment schemes, industrial visits, and work experience placements, as well as direct financial and other support for schools. This sort of activity was beginning before the Manpower Services Commission became involved, but since that time there has been a major reorientation of education and training, with a shift towards the new vocationalism and closer links between schools and industry (Walford *et al.*, 1988). Given that this has occurred in the vast majority of maintained secondary schools, and many primary schools, there is little reason why companies should wish to concentrate their efforts on CTCs rather than spread them far wider into the maintained sector. Indeed, there is every good reason for them wishing to continue to influence the bulk of mainstream schooling, where the financial and other investment may be smaller and the effect proportionally greater.

The argument used against this is that the CTCs should act as a catalyst for change in the maintained sector, as LEA schools will be forced to compete to provide a similar schooling experience. While there may be some truth in the claim that schools will try to compete – they will have to if they are to survive – their problem is that the competition is fundamentally unfair. The odds are stacked against the schools. CTCs, with massive capital funding from industry and government, cannot but offer better facilities. Had that funding been made available to local maintained schools, such that all children could benefit, rather than a select few, the facilities for science and technology teaching within the whole region could have been substantially improved.

Not only was there reluctance on the part of industry to sponsor the colleges, but also sites could not be found, even where financial support was forthcoming. The restriction to inner-city areas usually meant head-on conflict with the local Labour-controlled council. By December 1987 the original idea was obviously in trouble, for Kenneth Baker had announced that LEAs could run CTCs if they wished, and negotiations had started with several voluntary controlled schools to try to persuade them to change their status to that of a CTC. At the very last stages of the Education Reform Bill's passage through Parliament the CTC idea was broadened out to include the arts, technology, film, and video, as Richard Branson had volunteered some money to support such a college. In August 1988 it was announced that the idea might be extended even further, as Sir Philip Harris, head of the Harris Queensway group, was prepared to support a CTC which would include special facilities for dyslexic children in Croydon. At that point the plan involved the closure of a 1,000-pupil school against the opposition of the governors so that it could reopen in 1991 as a CTC.

The first city technology college, in Kingshurst, Solihull, opened in September 1987. The original plan was that twenty CTCs would open by 1990, but at the point when Kingshurst took its first intake of 180 pupils it seemed that there would be only four others by that time. Colleges at Nottingham and Middlesbrough were due in 1989, and by early 1989 four more colleges were due in 1990 at Bradford, Croydon, Gateshead, and Dartford. The Bradford college was given the go-ahead on transfer of local authority power to the Conservatives in May 1988, Croydon is to be the site of Richard Branson's CTC for the arts, Gateshead CTC is heavily supported by fundamentalist Christians, and Dartford involves the conversion of an existing school. It is a strange mixture.

By this time there was also growing concern about the proportion of the start-up costs of the new colleges which was being borne by the government. The original intention was that the private sector should supply all or a substantial part of the capital costs, but by September 1987 even Kenneth Baker had admitted that this was not realistic. At Solihull the cost of buildings and facilities has been about £9 million, £2.5 million of which had been given by private industry. This is a higher proportion of private finance than seems to be expected elsewhere, for, by 1989 £86 million had been set aside for the CTCs over a period of three years, and total donations pledged were £28 million. As such gifts are allowable against tax, the actual cost to the givers may be nearer £18 million, with the government giving another £10 million in lost tax revenue.

Grant maintained schools

The announcement of city technology colleges had shown that the government was prepared to consider dramatically new ways of funding schooling. It wished to see a decline in LEA power, a greater diversity of schools, including more private ones, more private funding, and greater choice of schools for parents. Once such a willingness to consider change had been made evident, several pressure groups pushed for a whole range of wider reforms. Of particular interest was a publication by the Hillgate Group in December 1986. The Hillgate Group is an informal gathering of right-wing intellectuals, including Baroness Caroline Cox, John Marks, and Roger Scruton. All have been very influential in arguing against comprehensive education (see Steedman, 1987), claiming that educational standards have fallen, and that children are being corrupted under the influence of left-wing teachers and LEAs (for example, Scruton *et al.*, 1985; Cox and Scruton, 1984). Their booklet *Whose Schools?* received considerable media attention in the December before the general election.

The main proposals put forward in *Whose Schools?* were that all schools should be owned by individual trusts, released from the control of local authorities, and funded by direct grant from central government. Schools, rather than LEAs, would then regarded as the employers of teachers. They also proposed that the CTC idea should be extended to cover a wider range of 'real educational objectives' – the government should take the initiative in educational standards. They proposed that schools should also be encouraged to seek finance from outside sources in order to improve facilities and offer better terms to their teachers, that a wide range of information should be published about each school to assist parents in their choice, and that head teachers should have control over the appointment of teachers. Many of these ideas were incorporated into the Educational Bill.

The Hillgate Group were not alone in pushing for more radical change. Similar pleas were put forward by the Institute of Economic Affairs, in the form of a booklet by Stuart Sexton (1987), and many within the Conservative Party believed that such changes might be an electoral benefit. Stuart Sexton's document was published in March by the Institute of Economic Affairs. It is of particular interest in the context of this book, for he sees the idea of allowing schools to opt out of LEA control as just the first step towards 'a form of privatization'. He envisages that schools should be allowed to charge for extras, but he pushes the idea of *per capita* funding from the state for the educational part. He recognizes that regional variations in *per capita* funding will have to be accepted in the short term, but that a national *per capita* figure should be introduced as soon as politically possible. He argues that, once parents have got used to the idea, they would be able to take that state subsidy as an 'educational credit' to any school, including private schools. Private schools would then flourish under market forces. While there are doubts as to whether Margaret Thatcher wishes to go this far – it would involve greater expenditure, at least in the short term – it is interesting to note that funding for the grant maintained schools is to be on a *per capita* basis linked to local LEA costs.

The grant maintained schools proposals were formally announced in May 1987, as part of the election campaign, and there was every sign that this particular part of the Conservative manifesto had been added at the last minute. During May Margaret Thatcher seemed to have a rather different view of the role of grant maintained schools from that of the Secretary of State. For example, she surprised Kenneth Baker and others by announcing that the schools would be able to raise extra funding and might be able to charge fees. The statement was withdrawn. Mrs Thatcher announced that, although schools would initially retain their original character, once independent they would be free to decide upon their own admissions policy. Schools would be able to select in the knowledge of pupils' record, national attainment test results, interviews, and written tests. Mr Baker denied that selection was being reintroduced and stated that changes of character might occur only in the long term. Mrs Thatcher thought that a vast number of schools would want to opt out, Kenneth Baker thought that only a small number would want to.

The immediate reaction was again one of hostility from many other quarters, and this was sustained during the passage of the Bill through Parliament. Most of those groups actively involved in education were against the idea, primarily because they saw it as a way of reintroducing selection and increasing the differences between facilities in individual schools. But the various bodies saw a variety of practical difficulties, as well as being opposed to the principle of the scheme. The consultation papers resulted in several million words of evidence and comment being received by the DES. It is highly unlikely that Kenneth Baker read more than a brief sample. According to Julian Haviland (1988), who edited and published a selection of the replies, opting out generated more criticism than any of the other proposals. Far from all of this was from the political left; for example, of twenty two Conservative authorities responding to the consultation documents, only six were in favour and the remaining sixteen were opposed in principle and highly critical in detail. Many of the local authorities saw the proposals as leading to an administrative nightmare at a time of falling rolls – they saw the possibility of schools which the LEA planned to close seeking grant maintained status, leading to an alternative school being chosen, which would then itself seek grant maintained status, and so on. The process of removing unwanted school places would thus be slowed down and the final result would be a network of schools which did not best serve the community as a whole. The Audit Commission backed this by pointing to the possibility of perpetuating a wasteful distribution of resources, and the retention of schools which could provide good education only at exaggerated cost (Haviland, 1988: 108). The Society of Education Officers also pointed to expected decreased efficiency and effectiveness.

Those organizations opposed to the idea included the National Association of Head Teachers, the National Union of Teachers, the Association of County Councils, and the Association of Metropolitan Authorities. The Roman Catholic Church and the Church of England both saw major problems, as did the Conservative Education Association, and at one point it looked as if a revolt of Conservative MPs would occur on this issue. Conservative shire counties were as concerned as the metropolitan boroughs. The Commission for Racial Equality was concerned about the possible effects on ethnic minorities, and various groups highlighted the lack of reference to children with special needs. This last point was dealt with in the final Act, where safeguards were included. The professional Association of Teachers objected to the scheme in the following way:

> The proposals in this consultative paper are based on a series of assumptions which we doubt: that there are a sufficiently large number of well-informed, well-intentioned and leisured people to provide suitable governors; that all parents make choices as to the administration of schools which are both wise and informed; that grant maintained schools will be at least as cost-effective as LEA maintained schools; that governors and parents are the people best able to improve the education service; that all schools will be improved if some of them acquire grant maintained status; that willingness to assume responsibility is the same as capacity to discharge it.
> [Haviland, 1988: 112]

Those few voices raised in support of the idea were often disappointed that the proposals did not go far enough. The Centre for Policy Studies, for example, wanted the scheme to encourage the setting up of new schools and permit them to opt in. They had new Christian and Muslim schools particularly in mind. The Conservative Family Campaign warmly welcomed the plan, but wanted to see the restrictions on a school changing its character removed. They also wanted schools to be able to charge fees:

> Autonomy means independence, and we do not for one moment believe that a vast majority of the schools which become grant

maintained would wish to become fully fledged independent private
schools with extremely high fees. They may however wish to offer
certain extras which may require greater funding than the government
feels willing to provide. They should therefore have the possibility
of charging fees.

[Haviland, 1988: 132]

This last possibility was exactly the long-term possibility which concerned
a large number of individuals and organizations.

In the event, the speed at which legislation was pushed through meant
that most of the criticisms were ignored rather than answered. The relevant sections on grant maintained schools in the Education Reform Act
are very little changed from those proposed in the consultation document. Governors of any county or voluntary secondary schools or of
a primary school with 300 or more pupils can apply for grant maintained
status. A ballot must be called if two meetings of the governors decide
to pursue an application. If more than half the parents vote, then a simple
majority will be binding; if not, a second vote must be called, which
will be binding. Once an application has been made, the Secretary of
State decides on each case individually. If grant maintained status is
granted the schools governing body will take over the school buildings
from the LEA and become fully responsible for them. Staff become
employed by the governing body, and responsible to it. Current expenditure will be paid by central government, but recovered from the LEA,
and will be calculated according to a formula which will also apply to
the LEA's schools. It will include the school's share of local council
advisory and central administration costs. The LEA will ramain responsible for just a few welfare services, such as educational psychologists,
careers service, the provision of transport, and the payment of clothing
allowances. Grant maintained schools will be subject to the national
curriculum.

In January 1988 the Centre for Policy Studies published a booklet
on grant maintained schools (Lawlor, 1988) which put forward the
benefits of grant maintained status in the following terms:

Grant Maintained schools will break the LEA monopoly of state
schools. Freed from the frustrations of local authority interference,
heads and governors will be able to shape their schools as they see
fit. They will choose and appoint the teachers. They will allocate funds
where they are needed, e.g. on books and equipment, and apply for
the services and support which they (not the local authority administra-
tors) consider best for their schools. They will be able to develop
the character of their schools, unhindered by continual requests for
form-filling and interference from the town hall. It is the head on
whom responsibility for the quality of a school falls. Under these

proposals he [*sic*] (and the governors) will have the power to meet
that responsibility.

[Lawlor, 1988]

After the Education Act became law the Grant Maintained Schools
Trust was established to promote and assist in the development of grant
maintained schools. It published a booklet, *The New Choice in Education* (1988), which gave some indication of what the benefits of grant
maintained status were expected to be. The main advantage is presented
as follows:

> Grant-maintained status gives schools, for the first time, freedom from
> local authority control, at no cost to parents. Many parents, governors
> and teachers believe that too many decisions are made by people who
> are too remote to have the best interest of individual schools at heart.
> This need no longer be the case. Grant-maintained status offers those
> directly involved the opportunity to decide how their schools are run.
> [Grant Maintained Schools Trust, 1988]

This booklet, which is designed to interest parents and governors in grant
maintained status, is a strangely insubstantial twelve-page glossy, with
only five pages of well spaced text. It actually seems unable to find many
positive advantages, and even admits that the Education Act's proposals
for local financial management, which are to be phased in by 1993, will
actually give schools most of the advantages of grant maintained status.

Nor is there much evidence that substantial numbers of people actually
want schools to opt out of local authority control. A MORI poll conducted
for the *Guardian* (9 February 1988) in January 1988 showed that only
18 per cent wanted to see any schools in their area opt out. Seventy-one
per cent wanted them to remain in local authority control. The Grant
Maintained Schools Trust document does, however, give some indication
of where grant maintained status might be popular. It states that:

> Grant-maintained status is primarily for those schools which have,
> over the years, built up a good reputation, able staff and the support
> of the communities. It will be attractive to schools which though
> flourishing and confident find their scope for development restricted.
> For them independence through grant-maintained status could be the
> next natural step.
> [Grant maintained Schools Trust, 1988]

But the booklet goes on to admit that the schools which may look
towards grant maintained status may also be those under threat of change
of character (which presumably means comprehensivization, but may
include closure), those suffering from interference by local authorities,
or those which feel better able to make use of resources spent centrally.

In other words, those schools which for one reason or another feel hard done by at the hands of their LEA or are under some threat are likely to seek to opt out. The parents of children who happen to be in a school at one particular time will thus be able to sabotage the plans of the democratically elected local authority for education of the area as whole. By April 1989 fifty-three schools had held ballots on opting out. Only thirty-nine of these votes had been in favour, including many schools scheduled for closure under LEA reorganization schemes. Just eight schools had been granted grant maintained status by the Secretary of State to start in September 1989.

When the Education Bill was passing through Parliament it seemed that there was considerable interest in opting out, but as time has passed much of this interest has evaporated. Some of the problems of independence have become more evident to schools, and also there has been a greater realization that local financial management might bring many of the perceived benefits of grant maintained status without the risks. Oddly, it is beginning to look as if the two most obvious pillars of the privatization process are going to be less important than had been expected. Instead, the greater power given to governing bodies and local financial management may become the key paths to a slower but more thorough privatization process.

Local financial management

The delegation of part of the LEA education budget to individual schools is far from new. LEAs have for many years given Heads the freedom to spend a proportion of the budget as they felt best suited their schools. Until recently, however, the amount of money involved was small and related to only a limited range of spending. In particular, such autonomy rarely included staff salaries, which are the major expenditure item of any schools. (Although ILEA did have such a scheme in 1973: Downes, 1988.) However, the last decade has seen a growth in the number of experiments where the range of expenditure included has been far greater than before. These schemes are variously called financial autonomy, local school management, local financial management, or some similar phrase. In Solihull a scheme was introduced in 1981 which has since been extended; it includes expenditure on teaching and non-teaching staff, as well as on buildings and maintenance. Heads are free to spend their budget more or less as they wish, and can carry forward any underspending to the next year (Humphrey and Thomas, 1986). In Solihull financial autonomy, as it is called there, was originally introduced as a cost-cutting exercise, and substantial savings were initially achieved. A new chairman of the Education Committee had the belief that, if the same sort of procedures were used to run schools as he used in running a small business, savings would result. As the former Director of Education, Colin Humphrey (1988) put it, 'Standard of service was about to become second fiddle to cost effectiveness.' Since 1985 the scheme has been run on a 'value for money' basis rather than as a cost reduction device, but future schools finance officers are warned that 'Reserves should be kept to a minimum safe level and other unspent funds clearly marked for projects – otherwise hard pressed Councils might see reserves as justification for education cuts' (p. 12).

Cambridgeshire introduced a fairly similar local financial management scheme in 1982, following on from earlier small-scale experiments. In this case the intention was not to cut costs, and the implementation of a central accounting system for the scheme has actually added to expenditure. Since 1987 the scheme has covered all forty six secondary schools and some primary schools in the county. Here the scheme was introduced in order to 'enable the Governors and Head of each school to make the most effective use of resources available to them and to give each Head flexibility within an agreed budget to manage the school' (Downes, 1988: 4). By 1987 more than twenty LEAs were involved in similar experiments or pilot schemes.

The Education Reform Act makes local financial management (LFM) compulsory for all secondary schools and primary schools of over 200 pupils. The governing body of each school will be given the responsibility for the financial management of the schools, delegated on a day-to-day basis to the Head. Governing bodies will become responsible for expenditure on staffing, books, and equipment, heat and light, cleaning and rates. They will also be allowed to provide meals if they can do so at the same or lower cost than the LEA service. LEAs will remain responsible for home-to-school transport, for providing advisory, inspection, and other services, and for the administration of pay, tax, and superannuation (Haviland, 1988: 136). The budget for each school will be calculated on a formula basis which will vary according to the number of pupils in the school and any special circumstances. It will include the vast majority of the running costs of the school, including all staff salaries – manual, technical, secretarial, and teaching staff. While teaching staff will still be formally employed by the LEA, the governors will be given the power to employ new staff within their budget and to sack staff, subject to the usual employment rights. Some changes were made to this part of the Education Reform Bill as it passed through Parliament. In particular, more safeguards were built in to ensure that teachers had the right to put their case to the governing body and seek an appeal in case of dismissal.

The pilot local financial management schemes already in operation have generally been popular with Heads and teaching staff. Heads have been faced with a higher work load and more responsibility, but in return have often felt better able to run thir school as they wished. Frustrations with LEAs over services and supplies have been eased. This general level of popularity led to there being a lower level of concern about the LFM changes in the Education Reform Act than about many of the other changes. While heavy and continued criticism was directed towards the grant maintained schools idea, a similar campaign was not directed towards LFM. Yet, when coupled with more open enrolment and far greater powers being given to governing bodies, both in the 1986 and in the 1988 Acts, there is actually very little difference between the new LFM schools and grant maintained schools.

There has been very little criticism of the basic idea of local financial management, but a great deal about the scale of the delegation of responsibility envisaged and the imposition of this by law. The concern centres on legislation where implementation is too fast and too extensive. One major problem highlighted by many of those responding to the consultation papers is that a satisfactory formula for funding has not yet been achieved in any of the pilot schemes, and may not be achievable. One of the points made by the Audit Commission and several of the local authority organizations is that local financial management will cost more to administer than the old system. The study team which wrote a Coopers & Lybrand report on LFM say that it is difficult to say whether LFM by itself will lead to net savings or net costs; 'the position will vary considerably between authorities. On balance we would be surprised if there were net savings' (Coopers & Lybrand, 1988). They stress that LFM is to be seen not as a means of reducing costs, but as a way of developing a more effective and responsive schools system. Schools would certainly be much better placed to get things done quickly, but would be rewarded with a heavier burden of administration.

Several other organizations have also expressed concern that there is an unrecognized need for a central pool for emergency and unplanned expenditure which it would be unreasonable to expect each school to plan for. As one of the LEAs which have already introduced LFM to a high degree, Cambridgeshire County Council's views are particularly interesting.

> Delegation to schools, as practised in Cambridgeshire and as outlined in the consultation paper, goes beyond financial matters. It is about local management of the whole school. Nevertheless there are some aspects of school education which demand an overview of educational needs and good practice which no one school can be expected to have. These are the proper concerns of the local education authority, and the proposals suffer from a failure to take account of some of them. The proposal that governors should be empowered to hire and fire heads and other staff makes a nonsense of the LEA's status as an employer.
>
> [Haviland, 1988: 147]

This concern with wider issues is one which should be seen in the light of related changes in open enrolment and in the powers of school governing bodies. Since the 1980 Education Act local education authorities have had to set upper limits for each of the schools in advance of parental choices being made. They have been able to take account of the long-term needs of the entire community by setting limits which were lower than the physical capacity of the individual schools, such that all schools in the LEA received a fair share of pupils. In this way a full curriculum could be maintained for pupils in all schools, and buildings put to the most effective use. The 1988 Act legislates such that admission limits have to be set at the 1979 levels, when pupil numbers in most LEAs were at a peak.

The intention is that popular schools will take in more children than the less popular schools, and schools will compete in the market place and either improve or be closed. However, once a shift has started to occur, the less popular schools will automatically receive less funding according to the LFM formula and be less able to compete. They will lose staff and possibly areas of the curriculum, and inevitably fall into a downward spiral. There is no guarantee that standards will be maintained. Differences between the schools will widen. Yet not all children will be able to attend the popular schools, for they will eventually become too popular, and attract more parents and children than there is accommodation for. Selection will thus become a necessity, whether the schools are nominally comprehensive or whatever. The major difference between opted-out schools and LEA maintained schools under the new regulations will be that the LEA could propose the closure or reorganization of an LEA school, but not of a grant maintained school. In practice an LEA school scheduled for closure might well then seek grant maintained status.

Cordingley and Wilby (1987), writing before the Act became law, point out that, taken together, the various changes amount to the introduction of a voucher system.

> The differences between what the government proposes and how a voucher system would operate are trivial. Under the latter, parents would receive a voucher, equivalent to the average annual cost of educating a child, which they could present to the school of their choice. The school would then redeem the voucher for cash from the government or local authority.
>
> The government's scheme works on exactly the same principle, except that there is no voucher. Instead parents simply present their child. Of course, there are limitations, but so would there be in any voucher system. For example parents will not get places if a school is full. Holding a voucher would make no difference any more than cash in the pocket will get you on to a bus or into a theatre that is full.
>
> [Cordingley and Wilby, 1987: 7]

101

This is an interesting analysis and one which highlights the full extent of the privatization process that has occurred as a result of the Education Reform Act. The idea of the educational voucher has been a central one for the radical right for many years, but vouchers have been too frequently attacked by those involved in education for the government to risk openly introducing them. Instead, it has followed the programme outlined by Stuart Sexton (1987) and 'privatized by stealth'. What is at present a direct grant could be renamed 'educational credit' or 'educational voucher', for parents are in the position of consumers picking and choosing in the market place.

The difficulty with Cordingley and Wilby's (1987) analogy is that we all know that money in the pocket *can* get us into a full theatre if we are prepared to supplement the ticket price, or can allow us to hire a taxi instead of a bus to travel wherever we want to go. Once popular schools are allowed to select children, there will be no orderly queue to get on the bus but, as with private medicine, affluent parents will ensure that their children are able to gain prime positions in the queue. Initially, this may be simply by showing that they are prepared to give their children an abundance of support (as with selection for CTCs), but Sexton's plan envisages that many parents will wish to 'top up' the value of their educational credit, and it will be hard for schools to resist selecting those parents who are most likely to do so. Full privatization of the education service is still some way off, but the Education Reform Act brings the possibility many steps closer.

Summary

This chapter has examined the major elements of the privatization process contained within the Education Reform Act of 1988. City technology colleges and grant maintained schools are radical initiatives which directly extend the private school sector. However, it is argued that, taken together, the changes with regard to open admissions, local financial management, and wider powers of governing bodies are very similar in effect. The Education Reform Act is a stage in the process of privatizing by stealth, and with little recognition the government has been able to introduce what amounts to a voucher system into schooling.

Chapter six

Choice and freedom or structured inequality?

We have seen that the 1988 Education Reform Act has made fundamental changes to the nature and structure of educational provision in England and Wales. The range of changes includes the national curriculum, with its associated testing and assessment procedures, more open enrolment, grant maintained schools, local financial management, and major changes in higher and further education. The main argument of this book has been that, although these developments may appear to be diverse, they are linked by the ideology of privatization.

It has been argued that the process of privatization in education has close similarities to that which has occurred in many areas of social and welfare services. In areas as varied as provision for old people, the National Health Service, and housing there has been a move away from public provision towards the private, with increasing differences in the quality of service offered in each of the sectors.

In all these areas, as with education, public provision developed only in the last hundred years or more. Before that time all these welfare and social services were in private hands – the affluent were generally able to buy their own high-quality services, while the poor were dependent upon what could be obtained through charity. As the century progressed, the state became increasingly involved in educational provision. There was a consequent decline in the private sector, due to amalgamation within the state maintained sector or as a result of competition, and it has become a small but still important part of the country's educational system. In chapters one and three it was shown that, although there is great diversity between the remaining private schools, it is possible for parents to buy privilege for their children if they choose wisely. Private education is not automatically 'better' than that in the maintained sector, but a careful selection of school can ensure that children are likely to be given an advantage in terms of facilities and opportunities for self-advancement, which can lead to examination success and entry into higher education and prestigious occupations.

In the first part of this century the Labour Party's main educational concern was with developing more provision within the state sector and encouraging greater access. The 1944 Education Act resulted in free secondary education for all, but within a state maintained tripartite system which offered different educational experiences for the children allocated to each type of school. It soon became evident that selection for these different types of school was heavily and unfairly related to social class, and that this led to unequal educational opportunities and lack of social mixing.

Comprehensive education was seen as the solution to many of the problems of the maintained sector and as a way of raising educational standards for all children. As this form of schooling became the firm policy of the Labour Party hostility to the remaining private sector grew. Private schools were seen as a deviation from the comprehensive ideal which had to be removed. The arguments used against selective education are essentially the same arguments that are used against private schooling, and, in turn, against the privatization process.

Six objections to private schools

Let us first review the main objections put forward against private schools. In a somewhat arbitrary way, they can be summarized in six points.

1. It is widely believed that it is possible to buy educational, social, and occupational advantages by attendance at the major private schools. We have seen that there is evidence that this belief is correct, although the advantages that can be gained are not as obvious as it might immediately seem, and are available only if parents choose wisely within the private sector. However, pupils at the major schools are likely to obtain an advantage in terms of A-level successes, and in terms of entry to university and higher education. This can lead in some cases to privileged access to occupations, but here the evidence is less clear. Evidence is also unclear on the question of whether or not such schooling and the 'old boy networks' that develop help in occupational success. We have seen that the advantages to be gained through private schools are not simply related to social class, and that there are substantial numbers of first-generation children in the major schools. However, those upper-class parents who have retained their position are able to use the private sector to help pass on their social privileges.

It is felt to be unfair that people should be able to buy these advantages. Children with wealthy parents already have many advantages; to be able to buy further privileges merely increases the inequalities in society.

2. Private education means that children of parents who are able and willing to pay fees are segregated from their peers who attend state maintained schools. Their understanding of society is thus narrow.

These educational divisions develop into, or at least reinforce, social and economic divisions in adulthood. It is argued that this is bad for both groups of children and for society as a whole. Those few children on scholarships who attend private schools are insufficient in number to ensure that the majority in such schools are able to come to an adequate understanding of our society. This is a particular problem where pupils from private schools do gain occupational success and become leaders of industry, commerce, the civil service, and politics, where they will have power over the majority of the population, of whom they have restricted knowledge and experience. A further important facet of this argument is that private schools are sometimes ethnically segregated, while we live in a multi-cultural society.

3. Parents who use the private sector are unlikely to fight for improvements in the maintained sector. Those parents who are prepared to pay fees are often strongly concerned about the quality of education available for their children. They are also often highly articulate, knowledgeable people of influence. These are exactly the sort of people who could successfully fight for further funding within the maintained sector, and who would do so if their children used it. Improvements to the general level of educational provision cost a great deal, and any increases have to be fought for in competition with other government spending priorities. Parents who use the private sector are unlikely to fight to see further expenditure on state maintained education.

4. It is argued that private schools harm the maintained sector by having an unfair distribution of scarce educational resources. We have seen that there is good evidence that the distribution of resources is not even. The major private schools are likely to have far better educational, sporting, and social facilities than most maintained schools. Although it might be argued that this is in itself unfair, the maintained schools would not automatically benefit in this context if there were no private schools. Teachers, however, are often scarce resources too. Shortage subject teachers such as physicists, mathematicians, and computer scientists can be tempted away from the maintained sector by higher salaries and better working conditions. The presence of a private sector can thus directly impoverish the maintained sector.

5. Parents are not always the best judge of what is good for their children. We have seen that some of those who use the private sector are probably choosing badly, for the worst private schools offer anything but advantage for the children who are sent to them. Some have poor facilities, poor teaching, and poor care. All private schools have to meet a minimum standards of safety and health, but HMI inspections are few and far between, and do not guarantee that high enough standards of teaching and learning are maintained. Other parents choose private schools which have high standards but which may be inappropriate for

the particular child. For example, a very 'sporty' school may be favoured by a father, but make life a misery for the son. Similarly, a school with a heavy emphasis on science or technology may be favoured by parents, but may be a bad choice from the child's point of view. A common problem that many private schools have to face is the parent who does not believe that his or her child is unsuited to higher education. A less highly academically pressured school might well be far better suited to the child. Parental choices can also have a detrimental narrowing effect on the schools themselves. Choices between schools have to be made on a restricted range of evidence, and there is a tendency for numerical data to form an important part of the comparative process. This can lead to a greater concentration on examination results at the expense of less quantifiable social and personal development issues.

6. The presence of private schools encourages the belief that education can be seen as an individual consumer commodity, where parents should be able to exercise freedom of choice between a variety of organizations providing the service. In practice, each child is not just an individual or a member of a family, but is also a member of society. That society enforces and funds schooling not just for the benefit of the child, but also because it recognizes that society as a whole gains from universal education, and from the transmission of some elements of common culture. Individual choices will not always coincide with what is best for society as a whole, and while individual choice is to be encouraged, freedom of action must be in part constrained by considerations of what is good for others within society.

Against privatization

I have argued that the major strand which draws together the various aspects of the Education Reform Act is the concept of privatization. While this is not the only basis of reforming zeal, it is by far the most important. Even many of the large number of new powers which the Secretary of State now holds can be seen as part of this privatization process, for they have often been introduced to help define the quality of the 'goods' which schools are to provide. The government is viewing itself as a consumer of schooling on behalf of society, and has introduced quality checks and controls to ensure that society's major demands are met. The prime example of this is the national curriculum and associated testing. Here as elsewhere, though, there is some degree of lack of coherence, as, logically, the national curriculum should be extended to all schools: but it is not mandatory within the private sector. Some of the new centralizing powers do also appear to be there just because there are conflicts within government about the extent to which privatization should occur.

While most of this chapter will concentrate on the objections to the privatization process evident in the Education Reform Act, it is worth recognizing that there are elements of the Act which are progressive. The introduction of the idea of a national curriculum, but not the testing, is a much needed reform. There will be differences of opinion about what should be included that national curriculum – for example, I would like to see anti-racism and anti-sexism as an integral part – but the concept is one which should be supported within a highly geographically mobile society. At present, without any national curriculum guidelines, a change of school can lead to severe problems of lack of continuity for a child.

An increase in the degree of local financial autonomy is also to be welcomed, for many small decisions are far better dealt with at the school level rather than through the bureaucratic processes of corporate management LEAs. Many of the petty frustrations of everyday teaching can be lessened through greater local financial delegation. The difficulty, of course, is in defining what the appropriate degree of delegation should be. The Education Reform Act goes further than is desirable, for it restricts the ability of an LEA to plan and to introduce LEA-wide policies. It also allows too great a level of freedom in the selection and payment of teaching and other staff, so that existing inequalities between schools can be amplified through pay differentials and payment for extra staff.

We saw in the last chapter that the principles behind CTCs, grant maintained schools, and local authority LFM schools are very similar, and that concern over the first two has obscured the privatization inherent in the third. A greater degree of local financial management is desirable, but the Act takes this to a level where all schools can begin to act as private schools. At this point selection and inequality of provision become inevitable.

City technology colleges were put forward as a way of improving technological education. They were designed to offer better facilities to a selected few, and also raise the quality of technological education elsewhere by way of example and competition between schools. The extension of the scheme to include technology for the arts, and to a college with special facilities for dyslexic children, shows that this is not their only purpose. As was made clear even in the original announcement by Kenneth Baker, CTCs are not simply about improving technological education, they are about establishing state funded schools independent of the LEAs. They are about making selection respectable again. They are about offering different educational experiences to selected children, and allowing vast differences in facilities to be provided within schools funded by the state. The Assisted Places Scheme was an attempt to both legitimize selection by ability and encourage the belief that private provision was superior to that of the state. The Aided Places Scheme for private music and ballet schools illustrated the belief that some children should be subsidized at a far higher level. City technology colleges took the privatization process one stage further.

Selection was a key aspect of the CTC idea, and it was important that parents and children were seen to compete for places. But selection was not to be on academic ability. At the time of the announcement, just before an election, it would have been too risky to announce that a new academically selective scheme was being introduced. It was possible to support the existing grammar schools, but several attempts to try to reintroduce LEA-wide selection had shown that many Conservative voters actually preferred their existing comprehensive systems. In Solihull, for example, the site of the first CTC, such an attempt had been made in 1983, but it had been overthrown largely as a result of pressure from middle-class actual and potential Tory voters who had ensured the success of their own children by buying into the 'correct' neighbourhoods serving popular comprehensive schools (Walford and Jones, 1986). Thus selection was to be based on such things as general aptitude, progress, and achievement in the primary school, and the parents' commitment to full-time education or training up to the age of 18. In other words, those children and parents who are keen, enthusiastic, and concerned about education are likely to be selected. Those very parents who might fight to maintain adequate standards of education within the maintained sector are to be selected out of it and their children given excellent facilities in state funded private schools. Those children who are interested in school and well motivated, who might encourage a class, and give added motivation to teachers, are to be removed from the local authority sector. City technology colleges thus act in a similar way to other private schools, and remove the very parents who might be expected to care most about their children's education. They also segregate these children from the majority of other children. Even their longer school hours act to help discourage social mixing outside school time.

City technology colleges also illustrate a clear example of the fourth objection to private schools. In the main, teachers in CTCs are likely to be appointed from positions in the maintained sector. The colleges will be able to attract teachers because of the excellent facilities that will be available and because the children have been selected to be highly motivated. Being part of such a new school would also be, in itself, exciting and challenging. Yet many of the teachers who would move to the CTCs are exactly those in shortage subjects in the maintained sector. Local authority schools may find themselves without a single physicist or computer specialist while the nearby CTC attracts a handful.

For the sake of the individual children involved it is to be hoped that CTC selection procedures will be good enough to ensure that no children without at least some leaning towards science and technology will be selected. But the selection process is in itself damaging to the local authority schools. Those children who are not selected will deem themselves to have 'failed' in the same way as in the old tripartite system. As parents will also play a part in the selection process, they too will feel the pain of failure. The local authority schools thus have to deal with the fact that they are 'second choice' and already deemed to be inferior. The selection process is also open to the same difficulties of accuracy of selection, training for interview, and no allowance being made for late developers that were present in the old 11+ examinations (Ford, 1969). In this case, though, some children will suffer the disadvantage that their parents will play a part in the actual selection procedure. Highly suitable children will fail to be selected simply because their parents failed to be interested enough to apply for a place.

At the level of the individual child, there is little doubt that the quality of education received in a CTC should be higher than in most local authority schools. While the quality of schooling is not directly related to funding levels, the degree of investment and support given to the CTCs must at least make schooling more enjoyable. The teachers in such schools are likely to be enthusiastic, and be involved in new developments. The problem is that *all* children are important and not just those children whose parents have learnt to play the new market in schooling most effectively. If excellent facilities are deemed necessary for some, then they should be deemed necessary for all. To allow and encourage the growth of inequality in provision is to harm the majority of schools in the maintained sector.

The main difference between grant maintained schools and CTCs is that there will be no injection of new money to improve facilities. Whether these schools survive is likely to depend largely on the reasons why they originally opted for grant maintained status. Where the grant maintained school was a popular LEA school, it is likely already to have better facilities than those around it. In some LEAs there are considerable differences in the funding made available to individual schools and in the capital expenditure which has been devoted to the school over the years. Schools which are now, or were previously, grammar schools often have better facilities than those which are or were secondary modern schools. Further, popular schools are likely to enjoy a greater level of financial support from parents, which allows the differences in activities and facilities to grow. Popularity is thus likely to lead to greater popularity, and, bar any scandals, a popular school which opts out should expect to gradually increase the numbers of pupils applying to it. Selection becomes inevitable and, although the Education Reform Act stipulates that grant maintained schools must retain their character for several years and change it only if the Secretary of State agrees, selection is unlikely to be on a random basis.

Faced with too many parents wishing their children to attend a comprehensive grant maintained school, selection procedures would probably involve some form of interview between the parents, children, and head teacher. Selection would probably be organized so that a spread of the local ability range would be taken, but within each sector of that ability range other factors would be taken into consideration. No doubt, as with the CTCs, this would include parental attitudes and the degree of support which the schools could expect from the parent. Some Heads might find themselves influenced by the financial support which parents were able to donate to the school. It is difficult to believe that middle-class children would not find themselves at an advantage over those from working-class backgrounds, with greater social class inequality and segregation as the result.

Popular grant maintained schools would also be able to attract good teachers simply because they could offer better facilities and well motivated children. Grant maintained schools with sufficient additional parental funding could also offer higher salaries to specialist teachers, or provide additional technical support staff to help teachers in their work. All this would increase the advantages of the grant maintained schools, directly impoverish LEA maintained schools, and accentuate the differences between schools.

On the other hand, a grant maintained school which opted for such status because it was under threat of closure, and where it was not a popular school, could not expect to do well. Opting out could have the effect of making parents more involved in the school, but this would be unlikely to be to such an extent that a turn-round occurred.

Under local financial management, with the associated abolition of 'arbitrary' admission levels, all schools will find themselves in a similar competitive situation. Those which are popular will receive additional help within their budget from the LEA on a *per capita* basis and from heavily involved parents, while those with fewer pupils will be less able to fulfil their obligations. Selection for schools will develop, with those children not able to attend their first-choice school deeming themselves failures. The government sees such differentiation within the school system as an inevitable consequence and determinant of freedom of choice. The market principle means that those children already from disadvantaged homes will probably find themselves at an even greater disadvantage, while those already having considerable advantages will probably be rewarded with further privileges.

That this is the 'probable' outcome is largely because it is not clear that all parents actually make the best decisions for their children, even where they are well informed. One of the aspects which make a school popular is high levels of examination success, yet we saw in chapter three that examination success is related to the ability of the school intake as much as to what goes on in the school. Without a knowledge of the range of abilities of the children selected for a school it is impossible to draw meaningful comparisons between schools. Publication of impressive GCSE and A-level results is meaningless without additional information. Those schools with what appear to be poor examination results may actually be giving better 'added value' than those with what appear to be excellent results. In this situation, parents are likely to choose unwisely, and the more effective school, in this narrow examination-based sense, may eventually be forced to close.

Individual parental choices made on a free-market principle are also unlikely to lead to an educational system which is in the best interests of society as a whole. Not only is it likely that schools will become more class differentiated, there is also the prospect of schools becoming segregated on ethnic lines. It is widely believed that a greater degree of parental choice will mean that many white parents will not send their children to schools where there is a large proportion of black or Asian children. On a television programme in November 1987 Baroness Hooper, one of the Ministers of Education, accepted that parents might well use their freedom of choice in a way which could lead to some schools in practice being for black children only, while others were for whites only. She was reported as saying, 'If we are offering freedom of choice to parents we must allow that choice to operate. If it ends up with a segregated system – then so be it' (quoted in the *Guardian*, 14 November 1987).

That this is a real possibility is backed by a Harris poll of parents in the Home Counties, conducted at about the same time, which found that 37 per cent of inner London parents supported the idea of racially segregated schools. In contrast only 20 per cent of Hindu parents, 17 per cent of Sikh parents, and 15 per cent of Muslim parents thought that it was important that their children attended a schools where the majority of pupils were from their own group. The United States has struggled for decades to try to ensure that schools desegregate, and so encourage greater equality of opportunity and social mixing. In Britain it seems that segregated schooling is just the 'price that society must pay' in order to increase individual parental choice.

What does the future hold?

The Education Reform Act is a stepping stone on the path towards privatization of the education service. We do not yet know how far down that path the government wishes to go. However, there are indications that this is just a brief resting place before stepping onward.

One of the places where these indications may be seen is in the publications of the various organizations which have been pressing for privatization, and which have already had a major influence on present government policy. For example, following their radical manifesto

111

Whose Schools? the Hillgate Group (1987) produced a response to
the government's consultation papers. They welcomed the proposals for
opting out but recommended 'certain modifications, one of which
involves a substantial further move towards fully independent schools'
(p. 34). They wish to see grant maintained schools able to change their
type (e.g. from comprehensive to grammar) after just one year, rather
than the minimum of five contained in the Act. They want teachers'
salaries to be determined locally by the governors and not in any way
restricted by national salary scales. The Act just gives flexibility within
the terms of the 1987 Teachers' Pay and Conditions Act. They also want
schools to be able to employ non-qualified people as teachers if they
wish. They encourage the voluntary schools to opt out of Church control
and become independent because grant maintained status will give better
funding, with 100 per cent capital expenditure being covered rather
than 85 per cent under the voluntary schools agreements. The group
also calls for a broadening of the CTC concept to include physical
education, humanities, business, agriculture, and many other specialist
areas.

The paper's most important suggestion on grant maintained schools
is that certain existing or new private schools should be able to opt into
the maintained sector as grant maintained schools. Included in this
proposal is the idea that some of these schools might still wish to charge
fees on top of the government grant. Such schools might include existing
or new Muslim and Seventh Day Adventist schools, which would in practice mean state funding for ethnically segregated schools.

The Hillgate Group also make similar proposals on local financial
management which are aimed at moving further towards a fully privatized
educational system. They want to see a greater emphasis on permanent
financial delegation, extension of the plan to all schools, including those
with fewer than 200 pupils, and more information made available about
individual school budgets. The aim of all these changes is to move towards
a voucher system. They state:

> All the initiatives included in the new Education Bill are compatible
> with the establishment, within the lifetime of this Parliament, of a
> nationally recognised pupil entitlement, which would cover the full
> cost of providing education for each pupil. . . . Once the pupil
> entitlement has been established, it would be both easy and desirable
> to make it available not to schools, but directly to parents, to
> be used in any school – LEA, grant maintained, Direct Grant or
> independent . . .
>
> It will perhaps be objected that such policies will subsidise the rich,
> or lead to an initial rise in public expenditure. If this is thought
> objectionable, then it is perfectly possible to provide a smaller

entitlement (needing to be topped up by parents) to those choosing independent schools . . .

[Hillgate Group, 1987: 42]

Such ideas are in line with Stuart Sexton's plans for adopting 'a step
by step approach to the eventual introduction of a ''market system'', of
a system truly based on the supremacy of parental choice, the supremacy
of purchasing power' (1987: 11). Anthony Flew (1988), who is another
contributor to the Institute of Economic Affairs publications, proposes
a tax credit system, which is 'but another interim step towards the eventual
utopia of all schools being independent, and a voucher system to pay for
them'. But vouchers do not guarantee entry to a chosen school, they merely
ensure that popular schools are able to select the children and parents they
wish, while the unselected 'failures' are consigned to second-rate schools.

Such selection of pupils is also in accord with ideas prevalent within
the Department of Education and Science. Brian Simon (1988) brings to
our attention some of the work of Stewart Ranson (1984), who interviewed
some senior officials in the department. One official explained that in terms
of long-term strategy for the system:

> There has to be selection because we are beginning to create aspirations
> which society cannot match. In some ways this points to the success
> of education in contrast to the public mythology which has been created.
> When young people drop off the education production line and cannot
> find work at all, or work which meets their abilities and expectations,
> then we are creating frustration with perhaps disturbing consequences.
> We have to select: to ration the educational opportunities so that socie-
> ty can cope with the output of education.

[Ranson, 1984]

Rarely has the case in favour of greater inequality in education been put
so clearly!

All these groups have had a great influence in the past and there is little
reason to expect their influence to decline. The unstated end of such a
process would be a gradation of educational provision tailored according
to class and ability to pay, with some adjustments being made for high-
ability working-class children. Once vocal, concerned, and influential
parents have been removed from the LEA system the basic level of
educational entitlement would automatically fall, and top-up payments
would become a necessity for an acceptable level of service. Many parents
have already become used to this idea through voluntary giving and
covenants, and it will be a small step to turn this into a fee.

The long-term aim, then, is a blurring of the boundaries between private
and state provision. There will still be a minimum level of

113

provision available free for all children, but those who are able and willing to pay for a more advantageous education would do so largely according to the depth of their pockets. At the top of the hierarchy would be the HMC and GSA schools, demanding a high top-up fee from most of their customers, but offering a number of scholarships to highly able children from parents unable to pay. Next would come a range of grant maintained schools and lower-ranking private schools, with lower fees according to parental means; and last would be those schools providing schooling in return for the educational entitlement only. Not all this last group of schools would be LEA-run, for within a market such as is envisaged new private schools would open to cater for this last group as well – maybe on a profit-making basis. After all, if prisons can be run on a profit-making basis, so too can schools!

The above description does not imply that there will be three distinct types of school, on the tripartite model, or five types, or whatever. The essence of the plan is that there should be a continuum and diversity of different forms of provision, which would build upon the diversity already within the private sector. Parents would be able to choose a form of education to match their aspirations and finances, in exactly the same way that they can now choose which restaurant to eat in.

While this would appear to be the long-term plan, there are a few indications that the government is not yet prepared to go this far. One specific example is that the proposal to enable new or existing schools to opt into grant maintained status was specifically rejected, as was an amendment to support English schools abroad, which are used primarily by British people working overseas. There are two possible reasons for this. The first is simply that the cost of allowing such a change could be too high. It is certain that many of the old direct grant schools would welcome such a possibility, as would a number of newer private day schools. Several private Muslim schools which have tried unsuccessfully to achieve voluntary aided status have indicated their desire to opt in, as has a group of forty-one evangelical Christian schools and the Seventh Day Adventist John Loughborough Schools in Haringey (Sutcliffe, 1988a). To bring all these schools into the maintained sector would be a very significant increase in educational expenditure.

The second possible reason for rejecting opting in is simply that the time is not yet right for such a move. Once the grant maintained schools have developed, such a change will appear inevitable.

A further somewhat promising sign concerns the sections of the Education Reform Act which deal with charging for 'extras' in maintained schools. In chapter four we saw that donations to maintained schools have now become common, as has charging for 'extras' such as individual music lessons, sporting activities, visits, the ingredients for home economics, and the materials for art and design. The boundary between donations and charges has become blurred, such that many schools now expect donations to be given for a variety of activities. As the Education Reform Bill passed through Parliament the government decided to clarify this situation by adding some new clauses. At that point there was general concern that this would mean that more of what had been thought of as essentials in the free education service were to be charged for. In practice, and as the draft DES circular of August 1988 makes clear, there has been a considerable tightening of what schools can charge for. They will no longer be able to charge for woodwork or cookery materials, or for any work connected with public examinations. Examination entry fees can be recovered only where 'the pupil fails without good reason' to meet syllabus requirements. Schools can ask for money for visits to such places as theatres and museums, but cannot exclude a child if the parents do not pay. Such a strengthening of the idea of free education is not in accord with the general thrust towards privatization, although it could be seen as an attempt to ensure that the minimum standard of provision is acceptably high.

While these two areas do indicate that the government is not yet ready to move to a fully privatized system, we should not be misled. The long-term aim remains one of encouraging and supporting inequality and selection in education. As the DES official interviewed by Ranson put it:

> We are in a period of considerable social change. There may be social unrest, but we can cope with the Toxteths. But if we have a highly educated and idle population we may possibly anticipate more serious social conflict. People must be educated once more to know their place.
>
> [Ranson, 1984]

What should be done?

The context

The Education Reform Act focuses on the idea of privatization. Parental choice within a market of diverse schools will ensure that inequality and selection will soon become the major characteristics of British education. Yet this is the very opposite of what our society requires. We need a free, state-maintained system where a high standard of education is available to all children, and where there is equality of opportunity. We need a well educated population in order to strengthen democracy, provide a skilled and knowledgeable labour force, and for personal self-development. The rights and freedoms of minorities need to be protected,

115

but society must ensure that those rights and freedoms do not infringe those of others. In particular, the educational system must be consistent with the creation of a harmonious and just society.

It is going to be very difficult indeed to change the direction in which the educational system is heading. The first necessity is to recognize that the educational system which existed prior to the 1988 Education Reform Act was far from offering equality of opportunity and that inequality was a major feature. Stephen Ball (1988) goes as far as to say that 'the so-called comprehensive reform never really happened', and that the real change that occurred after the 1960s was a concealment of the divisions and inequalities in education, rendering them more complex and less visible.

For example, we may well have a maintained system which is very largely comprehensive in name, but this is far from the same as being comprehensive in fact. In various LEAs, state maintained grammar schools exist alongside so-called comprehensive schools, but even where all LEA schools are comprehensive there can be major differences between schools.

The extent of these differences can sometimes be judged when attempts are made to effect changes in an existing comprehensive system. As indicated earlier, a good example occurred in 1983, when the Conservative Education Committee in Solihull attempted to reintroduce selective education. Solihull is a metropolitan borough adjoining Birmingham, which can be crudely divided into two areas – the working-class north and the affluent, middle-class south. The proposals for selection met with fierce opposition from both Labour and Conservative supporters, but it was the force of middle-class parents in the south which finally ensured that the comprehensive system was retained.

> Arguments about social and educational equality were simply out of place in a comprehensive system based on catchment areas which served to ensure that local schools, or even 'community schools', meant schools serving a relatively homogeneous social class intake. Children from the affluent middle-class were well catered for. In addition to their strong parental support and stocks of cultural capital, the active parent–associations had ensured that any necessary extras were provided. These schools were successful and efficient and would ensure that there was a high chance of adequate certification to legitimate social class reproduction. There was certainly no social mixing with the Birmingham overspill children living in the north of the borough.
>
> [Walford and Jones, 1986: 251]

The existing system meant that parents could ensure that their children went to a good comprehensive school simply by buying a house in the catchment area. The reintroduction of selection would have meant that some of these middle-class children would have been at risk of not being chosen for the selective schools.

The existence of voluntary schools is a further long-standing cause of inequality within the maintained system. About 20 per cent of the pupils in the maintained sector are in schools owned and controlled other than by the LEA. We saw in chapter two that the majority of Roman Catholic, Church of England, Jewish, Methodists, and non-denominational schools were integrated into the maintained system as it developed. The religious voluntary schools are selective in that they show a preference for children from one particular faith, but research by Bernadette O'Keeffe (1986) indicates that parents seek more than just a religiously grounded education for their children in these schools. She shows that there is a tendency towards educational and social advantage being available in them, and that there is a social class bias in their intake. The state now pays more than 99 per cent of the costs of voluntary schools but, whether by intention or design, they have often acted in opposition to LEA comprehensive intentions.

Finally, of course, the private sector still remains as the major way by which parents can buy advantage for their children.

Clearly, if we wish to build a fair and just educational system we would not start from here! Ideally, we would probably wish all schools to be owned and maintained by the state, and would, like the USA, establish a separation of state and religion to eliminate the inequalities inherent in any system which allows selection for Church schools. But, like it or not, we have to start from where we are – just after passing a major Education Act which is potentially very harmful in many of its measures.

If the first step is to recognize that the educational system prior to 1988 had major failings, the second is to accept that many of the changes within the 1988 Act are virtually irrevocable. We shall soon have an educational system where there is limited state support for pupils in some traditional private schools (APS), and full state support for pupils in some new special private schools (CTCs), in a diversity of semi-private schools (grant maintained), and in largely autonomous LEA schools. Diversity of ownership of schools funded by the state is already a *fait accompli*, and it is going to become politically very difficult to change. Parental choice is here to stay.

Diversity of ownership of state maintained schools need not, in itself, be a major concern. It might well be best to accept this and build upon it, for ownership actually makes very little difference – what is important is the degree of regulation attached to the receipt of state funding. For example, in the Netherlands some 72 per cent of secondary and 70 per cent of primary schools are private. Most are owned by the Catholic or

Protestant Churches, but some are independent. These schools are fully supported by the state, but are highly regulated such that central government pays most of the costs directly, including teachers' salaries on fixed scales. The government imposes substantial restrictions on the ability of schools to raise and spend extra funds, such that they are not allowed to supplement salaries or employ more teachers than calculated according to national staff/pupil ratios (James, 1989). Parents are able to choose between schools which differ in their teaching methods and ethos but which have a basic parity in terms of facilities and staffing.

The Dutch system is far from perfect – there is still a tendency towards social exclusivity, and there is insufficient local control – but it does illustrate that a diversity of school ownership and ethos is possible, without there necessarily being gross inequality. Indeed, it is possible to conceive of a system with in-built variety between schools which can actually increase social mixing. The magnet schools in the USA were introduced specifically with this purpose in mind. Cooper (1987) outlines one scheme of magnet schools in Kansas City which was carefully designed so that inequalities between schools were minimized. Every school was made 'special' in some way, such that all attracted a mix of children from various social and ethnic groups. Some schools were magnets in communications and writing, while others specialized in the performing and visual arts, science and maths, law and public service, business technology, and so on. The process of implementation was expensive, but such a system does have the advantage of offering choice in a situation where there are no 'sink schools' taking just those who fail to be selected for other schools.

The proposals

The proposals offered here are not a complete programme, but do offer some realistic ideas which aim at a fairer, less socially divisive, and higher-quality education for all. They build upon the best aspects of magnet schools, but within a highly regulated framework which allows local accountability.

1. *Private schools*. One of the major dangers to high-quality educational provision for all children is that the parents who are most likely and most able to press for good state maintained provision are able to opt out. Privatization blurs the boundary between state maintained and private provision. It is unrealistic to believe that the private schools can be abolished. This has occurred elsewhere only in authoritarian state regimes, and that is not a desirable path to follow. It is debatable whether it is a fundamental right for parents to be able to use private education for their children where this right may conflict with the rights of others, but it would appear that such may well be the case under the European

Convention on Human Rights (Lester and Pannick, 1987). In practical terms it makes little difference, for it is always going to be possible for parents to pay for private tuition if private schools are abolished. Those with sufficient money will always be able to opt out. For example, it could be expected that English schools in continental Europe would thrive if private schools were abolished here.

If private education cannot be abolished, it is most important that the remaining private schools are treated as a distinct group, separate from the maintained sector. All government support for the private schools should cease, so that the number of private schools will reduce. The various state maintained private schools would also compete with the fee-paying schools, and lead to some closures. This would result in a small, but elite, private sector but one to which only the very affluent would be able to aspire. All other parents would thus focus their attention on supporting and improving the maintained sector.

Private schools prepared to accept the high degree of regulation envisaged for the receipt of state grants should be allowed to opt in. Additionally a few of the grant maintained schools may wish to try to opt out and become fee-paying schools but, on the whole, the shifts would probably lead to a gradual reduction in the non-maintained private sector.

2. *The national curriculum* should be extended to all schools. Pupils in private schools as well as state schools should be subject to the same basic curriculum for the majority of their schooling. This curriculum should include moral and social aspects as appropriate for a multi-cultural society.

3. *Local financial management* should be retained, but LEAs should be given greater freedom to adjust the overall amount given to each school. Schools are funded by society as a whole, and not just by those parents of children who happen to be attending the school at any one time. It is thus appropriate that the representatives of the local society (i.e. the local authority) should have an effective say in how finance is allocated. Local authorities should distribute money such that those schools with children with the greatest social and educational needs receive the most support. This could be done to a formula if necessary. All schools receiving state grants should receive them through the LEAs so that such adjustments could be made. Central government would ensure that there was broadly equal funding in education between LEAs.

4. *Parental choice*. At the primary level, most parents would choose the local school provided that it offered high-quality schooling. Local authorities should be given the power to give higher budgetary allocations to schools with the greatest social and educational needs such that more schools become equally attractive to parents. Parents should retain the freedom to state a choice, so as to take personal factors into account. In urban areas, in particular, it would be possible for there to be a

119

diversity of ownership, style, and ethos of the schools. At the secondary-level, subject to the national curriculum, which would occupy most of the day, there is also room for diversity in the size, style, and ethos of schools. The magnet school concept could be used to encourage social and ethnic mixing of children and their parents. Schools could have magnets in art, drama, technology, sport, or whatever. They could also vary in their teaching style and methods. The aim would be parity of esteem between the various schools, but it is accepted that this would be very difficult to achieve completely.

It would, however, be possible for LEAs to ensure that there was parity in resources available through differential budgets. Diversity of this type would encourage student motivation, and would not necessarily be socially divisive. Indeed, the intention would be to obtain a social mix at each of the schools. It is likely that magnet schools would operate effectively only in urban areas. In rural areas they would not encourage a greater level of social mixing than is already the case. Religious voluntary schools should be regarded as simply another type of magnet school, specializing in that particular religious orientation. All schools receiving state funding should do so through the LEAs, which would also be able to impose admissions limits to schools where it was in the interest of the local education system as a whole. At secondary level, choice of schools should actively include the child as well as the parents, and all children should be made aware of their right to state a preference.

5. *Selection*. Diversity becomes unjust only when one group has preferential access. Access to all schools must thus be on a random basis. There can be no selection of any kind, with the possible exception of children with special needs. Nor can there be any criteria (other than the gender of the child for some schools) which have to be met. To ensure equality of opportunity, this must include religious belief. Children of beliefs other than that of the school should still be fully eligible for entry to the school, but should be allowed to opt out of any religious practices. Parents and children together should be able to apply to any secondary school they wish, and selection of each intake should be on a purely random basis from those who wish to attend. Random selection is the only way that a diversity of schools will not automatically lead to a hierarchy of schools. To encourage a heterogeneous social intake it may be necessary to have gender, class, and ethnic group quotas. If there were many more pupils than places for one particular specialism, other schools could start to offer it as a magnet. Thus there would be responsiveness to demand, but not at an individual level. The fact that parents could not ensure that their child would gain access to a particular school would mean that it would be in their interest to fight for maintained education as a whole, rather than for one particular school. They would be

wise to support high-quality education in all schools, for they might not be able to get their first choice.

Random selection is a vital accompaniment of diversity and choice, if a hierarchy of schools is not to develop. Within any system where a preference for a particular school is expressed, and some schools are more popular than others, some parents are going to be disappointed. There is nothing unfair about selection being entirely a matter of luck – it is certainly preferable to a selection process where parental background inevitably plays a major part, and where those from deprived backgrounds are at an automatic disadvantage.

6. *Private support*. Industrial, business, and private donations should be encouraged as long as they lead to a net increase in the resources devoted to education. Where such donations, in money or in kind, are given to individual schools the LEA might feel that it should adjust all school budgets accordingly to compensate. The school would thus actually benefit only by a proportion of the gift, and all other local schools would benefit by the same amount. In these circumstances it would be logical for companies and other bodies to work with all the schools in the district rather than one. This is exactly what is already occurring in many areas through TVE Extension, and is to be encouraged. It would be central government's task to ensure broad equality of spending between LEAs.

The proposals outlined above would bring about a major reorientation of the educational system, yet none of them demands impracticable changes. For example, it would be largely an administrative matter to allow LEAs to fund the CTCs and grant maintained schools directly, rather than by the circuitous route of government providing funding and then claiming it back from the LEAs. The greater control and direction given to funding that is required at the local level is a simple development of local financial management. If necessary, a formula could be constructed which would deal with most cases of differential block funding to schools.

The only major change required is a prohibition of selection by any other than random means. This will be more difficult to implement for political reasons rather than practical ones, for parents may well feel that such a process of selection is unfair. Here the CTCs and grant maintained schools may gradually lead to a change of opinion, for in both cases selection is likely to be on unspecified and hidden criteria, and parents who fail to gain entry for their children may recognize that such selection is grossly unfair. An open system based on luck would be seen as preferable. Once such a process had become accepted, the actual results of such selection would become less significant, for parents would not allow substantial differences to develop between schools. There would then be, in fact, choice and feedom *without* structured inequality.

References

Aitkenhead, J. (1986) 'That dreadful school: the "free school" at Kilquhanity', *Resurgence* 118: 6–9.

Ascher, Kate (1987) *The Politics of Privatisation. Contracting out public services*, Basingstoke: Macmillan.

Association of Metropolitan Authorities (1987) *City Technology Colleges. A Speculative Investment*, London: AMA.

Baker, Nick (1987) 'In the black', *Times Educational Supplement*, 25 September, p. 26.

Ball, Stephen (1988) 'A comprehensive school in a pluralist world – division and inequalities', in Bernadette O'Keeffe (ed.) *Schools for Tomorrow*, Lewes: Falmer.

Bamford, T.W. (1967) *Rise of the Public Schools. A study of boys' public boarding schools in England and Wales form 1837 to the present day*, London: Nelson.

Batchelor, Meston (1981) *Cradle of Empire. A Preparatory School through Nine Reigns*, Chichester: Phillimore.

Boyd, David (1973) *Elites and their Education. The educational and social backgrounds of eight elite groups*, Slough: NFER.

Briggs, David R. (1983) *The Millstone Race. A Study in Private Education*, Maidenhead, private circulation.

Cameron, D. (1985) 'Public expenditure and economic performance in international perspective', in Rudolf Klein and Michael O'Higgins (eds) *The Future of Welfare*, Oxford: Blackwell.

Chandos, John (1984) *Boys Together. English public schools, 1800–1864*, London: Hutchinson.

Chevannes, Mel, and Reeves, Frank (1987) 'The black voluntary school movement: definition, context, and prospects', in Barry Troyna (ed.) *Racial Inequality in Education*, London: Tavistock.

Clarke, Peter (1987) 'The argument for privatisation', in Julia Neuberger (ed.) *Privatisation . . . Fair shares for all or selling the family silver?* Basingstoke: Macmillan.

Conservative Party (1983) *General Election Manifesto*, London: Conservative Party.

—— (1987) *The Next Moves Forward. The Conservative Manifesto*, London: Conservative Party.

Cooper, Bruce S. (1987) *Magnet Schools*, London: Institute of Economic Affairs.

Coopers & Lybrand (1988) *Local Management of Schools*, London: Coopers & Lybrand.

Cordingley, Philippa, and Wilby, Peter (1987) *Opting out of Mr Baker's Proposals*, Ginger Paper One, London: Education Reform Group.

Cox, Caroline, and Scruton, Roger (1984) *Peace Studies. A Critical Survey*, London: Institute for European Defence and Strategic Studies.

Crosland, C.A.R. (1956) *The Future of Socialism*, London: Jonathan Cape.

Dancy, John (1966) *The Public Schools and the Future*, London: Faber.

Delamont, Sara (1976a) 'The girls most likely to: cultural reproduction and Scottish elites', *Scottish Journal of Sociology* 1: 29–43.

—— (1976b) *Interaction in the Classroom*, London: Methuen.

—— (1984) 'Debs, dollies, swots, and weeds: classroom styles at St Luke's', in Geoffrey Walford (ed.) *British Public Schools. Policy and Practice*, Lewes: Falmer.

Dennison, S.R. (1984) *Choice in Education*, Hobart Paperback 19, London: Institute of Economic Affairs.

Department of Education and Science (1985) *Assisted Places at Independent Schools*, London: DES.

—— (1986a) *Report of Her Majesty's Inspectors on the Effects of Local Authority Expenditure Policies on Education Provision in England – 1985*, London: DES.

—— (1986b) *City Technology Colleges. A new choice of school*, London: DES.

—— (1987) *Statistics of Education. School Leavers, CSE and GCE 1986*, London: DES.

—— (1988) *Statistics of Education. Schools 1987*, London: DES.

de Zouche, Dorothy (1955) *Roedean School, 1885–1955*, Rottingdean, private circulation.

Douse, Mike (1985) 'The background of Assisted Places Scheme students', *Educational Studies* 11, 3: 211–17.

Dover Report (1983) *Report of the Committee on Undergraduate Admissions*, Oxford: Colleges Admissions Office.

Downes, Peter (ed.) (1988) *Local Financial Management in Schools*, Oxford: Blackwell.

Edwards, Anthony, Fitz, John, and Whitty, Geoff (1989) *The State and Private Education. An Examination of the Assisted Places Scheme*, Lewes: Falmer.

Eglin, Greg (1984) 'Public schools and the choice at 18+', in Geoffrey Walford (ed.) *British Public Schools. Policy and Practice*, Lewes: Falmer.

Fitz, John, Edwards, Anthony, and Whitty, Geoff (1986) 'Beneficiaries, benefits and costs: an investigation of the Assisted Places Scheme', *Research Papers in Education* 1, 3: 169–93.

Flemming Committee (1944) *The Public Schools and the General Education System*, London: HMSO.

Flew, Anthony (1988) *Education Tax Credits*, London: Institute of Economic Affairs.

Ford, Julienne (1969) *Social Class and the Comprehensive School*, London: Routledge & Kegan Paul.

Fox, Irene (1984) 'The demand for a public school education: a crisis of confidence in comprehensive schooling?' in Geoffrey Walford (ed.) *British Public Schools. Policy and Practice*, Lewes: Falmer.

—— (1985) *Private Schools and Public Issues*, London: Macmillan.

Franks Report (1966) *Report of the Commission of Inquiry into the University of Oxford* II, Oxford: Clarendon Press.

Gabbitas Truman & Thring (1987) *Attitudes of parents towards Independent Education. MORI summary findings*, press release, 11 November, London: Gabbitas Truman & Thring.

Gathorne-Hardy, Jonathan (1977) *The Public School Phenomenon*, London: Hodder & Stoughton; reprinted 1979, Harmondsworth: Penguin.

Ginn, Tony (1987) 'Vision for the school desk', *Guardian*, 11 June, p. 15.

Glass, G.V., Cohen, L.S., Smith, M.L., and Filby, N.N. (1982) *School Class Size. Research and Policy*, Beverly Hills: Sage.

Glennerster, Howard, and Wilson, Gail (1970) *Paying for Private Schools*, Harmondsworth: Allen Lane.

Grant Maintained Schools Trust (1988) *The new Choice in Education*, London: Grant Maintained Schools Trust.

Griffiths, Brian, and Murray, Hugh (1985) *Whose Business? An analysis of the failure of British business schools and a radical proposal for their privatisation*, Hobart Paper 102, London: Institute of Economic Affairs.

Griggs, Clive (1985) *Private Schools in Britain*, Lewes: Falmer.

Halsey, A.H. (1981) 'Democracy in education', *New Society* 28, May.

Halsey, A.H., Heath, A.F., and Ridge, J.M. (1980) *Origins and Destinations*, Oxford: Clarendon Press.

—— (1984) 'The political arithmetic of public schools', in Geoffrey Walford (ed.) *British Public Schools: Policy and Practice*, Lewes: Falmer.

Haviland, Julian (1988) *Take care, Mr Baker!* London: Fourth Estate.

Hillgate Group (1986) *Whose Schools? A Radical Manifesto*, London: Hillgate Group.

—— (1987) *The Reform of British Education. From Principles to Practice*, London: Claridge Press.

Honey, John R. de S. (1977) *Tom Brown's Universe. The Development of the Public School in the 19th Century*, London: Millington.

Humphrey, Colin, and Thomas, Hywel (1986) 'Delegating to schools', *Education* 12: 513–14.

Humphrey, Colin (1988) *Financial Autonomy in Solihull*, London: Institute for Economic Affairs.

Independent Schools Information Service (1988) *Annual Census, 1988*, London: ISIS.

ISIS Newsletter (1983) *Election Special*, London: ISIS.

ISIS News (1987) *Special Issue April 1987*, London: ISIS.

James, Estelle (1989) 'Benefits and costs of privatised public services: lessons from the Dutch system', in Geoffrey Walford (ed.) *Private*

Schools in Ten Countries: Policy and Practice, London: Routledge.
Johnson, Daphne (1987) *Private Schools and State Schools. Two systems or one?* Milton Keynes: Open University Press.
Jowel, Roger, and Witherspoon, Sharon (eds.) (1984) *British Social Attitudes. The 1984 report*, Aldershot: Gower.
— (1985) *British Social Attitudes. The 1985 report*, Aldershot: Gower.
Jowell, Roger, Witherspoon, Sharon, and Brook, Lindsay (eds.) (1986) *British Social Attitudes. The 1986 report*, Aldershot: Gower.
— (1987) *British Social Attitudes. The 1987 report*, Aldershot: Gower.
Judd, Judith (1987) 'Now it's learn as you pay', *Observer*, 18 October.
Kay, John, Mayer, Colin, and Thompson, David (eds.) (1986) *Privatisation and Regulation. The UK Experience*, Oxford: Clarendon Press.
Kinnock, Neil (1986) *Making our Way*, Oxford: Blackwell.
Kirkman, Susannah (1987) 'Sweet charity', *Observer*, 18 October.
Labour Party (1980) *Private Schools. A Labour Party Discussion Document*, London: Labour Party.
— (1981) *TUC–Labour Party Liaison Committee Statement on Private Schools*, London: Labour Party.
— (1983) *A New Hope for Britain. Labour's Manifesto, 1983*, London: Labour Party.
— (1986) *Freedom and Fairness*, London: Labour Party.
— (1987) *Britain will Win. Labour Manifesto, June 1987*, London: Labour Party.
Lamb, F., and Pickthorne, H. (1968) *Locked-up Daughters. A parent's look at girls' education and schools*, London: Hodder & Stoughton.
Lambert, Royston (1966) *The State and Boarding Education*, London: Methuen.
Lambert, Royston, Hipkin, John, and Stagg, Susan (1968) *New Wine in old Bottles*, Occasional Papers on Social Administration No. 28, London: Bell.
Lambert, Royston, and Millham, Spencer (1968) *The Hothouse Society*, London: Weidenfeld & Nicolson; reprinted 1974, Harmondsworth: Pelican.
Lambert, Royston (1975) *The Chance of a Lifetime? A study of boarding education*, London: Weidenfeld & Nicolson.
Lawlor, Sheila (1988) *Opting out. A guide to how and why*, London: Centre for Policy Studies.
Leinster-Mackay, Donald (1984) *The Rise of the English Prep School*, Lewes: Falmer.
— (1987) *The Educational World of Edward Thring*, Lewes: Falmer.
Lester, Anthony, and Pannick, David (1987) *Independent Schools. The Legal Case*, London: ISIS.
Lodge, Bert (1987) 'Comprehensives pose no handicap to young golfers', *Times Educational Supplement*, 3 July, p. 1.
MacDonald Fraser, George (1977) (ed.) *The World of the Public School*, London: Weidenfeld & Nicolson.
Mack, Edward C. (1941) *Public Schools and British Opinion since 1860*,

New York: Columbia University Press; reprinted 1973, New York: Octagon Books.

McLean, Martin (1985) 'Private supplementary schools and the ethnic challenge to state education in Britain', in C. Brock and W. Tulasiewicz (eds.) *Cultural Identity and Educational Policy*, Beckenham: Croom Helm.

Maitland, Nicky (1988) 'On course for new levels of knowledge', *The Sunday Times*, 17 April, p. B10.

Manpower Services Commission (1987) *The Funding of Vocational Education and Training*, Sheffield: MSC.

Metz, Mary Haywood (1986) *Different by Design. The context and character of three magnet schools*, London: Routledge & Kegan Paul.

Mishra, R. (1984) *The Welfare State in Crisis*, Brighton: Harvester Press.

Morrish, Ivor (1970) *Education since 1800*, London: Unwin.

Musgrave, Peter (1968) *Society and Education in England since 1800*, London: Methuen.

Neill, A.S. (1962) *Summerhill*, London: Gollancz; reprinted 1968, Harmondsworth: Pelican.

O'Connor, Maureen (1986) 'No room in the dorm.', *Guardian*, 20 September, 11.

Ogilvie, Vivian (1957) *The English Public School*, London: Batsford.

O'Keefe, Bernadette (1986) *Faith, Culture and the Dual System*, Lewes: Falmer.

Okely, Judith (1978) 'Privileged, schooled and finished: boarding education for girls' in Shirley Ardener (ed.) *Defining Females*, London: Croom Helm.

Ollerenshaw, Kathleen (1967) *The Girls' Schools*, London: Faber.

Papadakis, Elim, and Taylor-Gooby, Peter (1987) *The Private Provision of Public Welfare*, Brighton: Wheatsheaf.

Parents' Guide to Independent Schools (1988), eighth edition, 1988–9, London: School Fees Insurance Agency Educational Trust.

Pirie, Madsen (1985) *Privatization*, London: Adam Smith Institute.

Price, Mary, and Glenday, Nonita (1974) *Reluctant Revolutionaries. A century of headmistresses, 1874–1974*, London: Pitman.

Price, Paul (1986) 'Comprehensive reorganisation and the direct-grant grammar schools', in V.A. McClelland (ed.) *Private and Independent Education*, Aspects of Education 35, Hull: University of Hull Institute of Education.

Pring, Richard (1983) 'Privatisation in education', paper for RiCE (Right to Comprehensive Education), Exeter.

—— (1986) 'Privatization of education', in Rick Rogers (ed.) *Education and Social Class*, Lewes: Falmer.

—— (1987) 'Privatization in education', *Journal of Education Policy* 2, 4: 289–99; reprinted as 'privatisation' in *Educational Management and Administration* 16, 2 (1988): 85–96.

Public Schools Commission (1968) *First Report of the Public Schools Commission*, chair John Newsom, London: HMSO.

—— (1970a) *Second Report, 1: Report on Independent Day Schools and*

Direct Grant Grammar Schools, chair David Donaldson, London: HMSO.
—— (1970b) *Second Report, 3: Scotland*, chair T. Ewan Faulkner, London: HMSO.

Rae, John (1981) *The Public School Revolution. Britain's Independent Schools 1964–1979*, London: Faber.

Ranson, Stewart (1984) 'Towards a tertiary tripartism: new codes of social control and the 17+', in Patricia Broadfoot (ed.) *Selection, Certification and Control*, Lewes: Falmer.

Rawnsley, Andrew (1986) 'Backing the old school tie', *Guardian*, 27 May, p. 5.

Redpath, Bob, and Harvey, Barbara (1987) *Young People's Intentions to Enter Higher Education*, Office of Population Censuses and Surveys, Social Survey Division, London: HMSO.

Reid, Ivan (1986) *The Sociology of School and Education*, London: Fontana.

Rentoul, John (1987) 'Privatisation: the case against', in Julia Neuberger (ed.) *Privatisation . . . Fair shares for all or selling the family silver?* Basingstoke: Macmillan.

Reynolds, K.M. (1950) 'The school and its place in girls' education', in *The North London Collegiate, 1850–1950*, London: Oxford University Press.

Ritchie, Harry (1988) 'Edinburgh's elitism', *New Society* 27, May, pp. 36–8.

Robinson, Gordon (1971) *Private Schools and Public Policy*, Loughborough: Loughborough University of Technology.

Robson, Mark H., and Walford, Geoffrey (1988) 'U.K. tax policy and independent schools', *British Tax Review* 2: 38–54.

—— (1989) 'Independent schools and tax policy under Mrs Thatcher', *Journal of Education Policy* 4, 2: 149–62.

Salter, Brian, and Tapper, Ted (1985) *Power and Policy in Education. The case of independent schooling*, Lewes: Falmer.

Sampson, A. (1982) *The Changing Anatomy of Britain*, London: Hodder & Stoughton.

Scruton, R., Ellis-Jones, A., and O'Keeffe, D. (1985) *Education and Indoctrination*, London: Educational Research Centre.

SDP/Liberal Alliance (1987) *Britain United. The Time has Come. The SDP/Liberal Alliance Programme for Government*, London: SDP/Liberal Alliance.

Seldon, Arthur (1986) *The Riddle of the Voucher*, Hobart Paperback 21, London: Institute of Economic Affairs.

Sexton, Stuart (1987) *Our Schools. A Radical Policy*, London: Institute of Economic Affairs.

Shaw, G.K., and Blaug, M. (1988) 'The University of Buckingham after ten years: a tentative evaluation', *Higher Education Quarterly* 42, 1: 72–89.

Shaw, Len (ed.) (1986) *Gabbitas-Thring Guide to Independent Further Education*, London: Harper & Row.

Simon, Brian (1988) *Bending the Rules. The Baker 'reform' of education*,

London: Lawrence & Wishart.

Simon, Brian, and Bradley, Ian (1975) *The Victorian Public School*, Dublin: Gill & Macmillan.

Society of Education Officers (1979) 'SEO oppose assisted places scheme', *Education*, 2 November.

Steedman, Jane (1987) 'Longitudinal survey research into progress in secondary schools, based on the National Child Development Study', in Geoffrey Walford (ed.) *Doing Sociology of Education*, Lewes: Falmer.

Stillman, Andy, and Maychell, Karen (1986) *Choosing Schools. Parents, LEAs and the 1980 Education Act*, Windsor: NFER/Nelson.

Sutcliffe, Jeremy (1988a) 'Evangelical schools seek to opt out', *Times Educational Supplement*, 15 January, p. 7.

—— (1988b) 'High earners of independent means', *Times Educational Supplement*, 29 April, p. 1.

Tapper, Ted, and Salter, Brian (1986) 'The Assisted Places Scheme: a policy evaluation', *Journal of Education Policy* 1, 4: 315–30.

Tuck, Dinah (1988) 'Local financial management', *Educational Management and Administration* 16, 2: 140–8.

Tutt, N. (1985) *The Tax Raiders. The Rossminster Affair*, London: Financial Training Publications.

Wakeford, John (1969) *The Cloistered Elite. A sociological analysis of the English public boarding school*, London: Macmillan.

Walford, Geoffrey (1983) 'Girls in boys' public schools: a prelude to further research', *British Journal of Sociology of Education* 4, 1: 39–54.

—— (1984) 'The changing professionalism of public school teachers', in Geoffrey Walford (ed.) *British Public Schools: Policy and Practice*, Lewes: Falmer.

—— (1986a) *Life in Public Schools*, London: Methuen.

—— (1986b) 'Ruling-class classification and framing', *British Educational Research Journal* 12, 2: 183–95.

—— (1987a) 'How dependent is the independent sector?' *Oxford Review of Education* 13, 3: 275–96.

—— (1987b) 'How important is the independent sector in Scotland?' *Scottish Educational Review* 19, 3: 108–21.

—— (1987c) (ed.) *Doing Sociology of Education*, Lewes: Falmer.

—— (1987d) *Restructuring Universities. Politics and Power in the Management of Change*, Beckenham: Croom Helm.

—— (1988a) 'The Scottish Assisted Places Scheme: a comparative study of the origins, nature and practice of the APS in Scotland, England and Wales', *Journal of Education Policy* 3, 2: 137–53.

—— (1988b) 'The privatisation of British higher education', *European Journal of Education* 23, 1/2: 47–64.

—— (1988c) 'Training the elite – for education, training and jobs', *Collected Original Resources in Education* 12, 1.

—— (1988d) 'Bullying in public schools: myth and reality' in Delwyn P. Tattum and David A. Lane (eds) *Bullying in Schools*, London: Trentham Books.

—— (1989) (ed.) *Private Schools in Ten Countries: Policy and Practice*, London: Routledge.

Walford, Geoffrey, and Jones, Sian (1986) 'The Solihull adventure: an attempt to reintroduce selective schooling', *Journal of Education Policy* 1, 3: 239–53.

Walford, Geoffrey, Purvis, June, and Pollard, Andrew (1988) 'Ethnography, policy and the emergence of the new vocationalism', in Andrew Pollard, June Purvis, and Geoffrey Walford (eds.) *Education, Training and the New Vocationalism. Experience and policy*, Milton Keynes: Open University Press.

Wallace, Wendy (1988) 'God's own office work', *Times Educational Supplement*, 19 February, p. 25.

Weinberg, Ian (1967) *The English Public Schools. The Sociology of Elite Education*, New York: Atherton Press.

Whitty, Geoff, and Edwards, Tony (1984) 'Evaluating policy change: the Assisted Places Scheme', in Geoffrey Walford (ed.) *British Public Schools. Policy and Practice*, Lewes: Falmer.

Whitty, Geoff, Edwards, Tony, and Fitz, John (1989) 'Private schools in England and Wales', in Geoffrey Walford (ed.) *Private Schools in Ten Countries. Policy and Practice*, London: Routledge.

Wilkinson, Richard W. (1986) 'The Assisted Places Scheme', in V.A. McClelland (ed.) *Private and Independent Education*, Aspects of Education 35, Hull: University of Hull Institute of Education.

Wilkinson, Rupert (1964) *The Prefects. British Leadership and the Public School Tradition*, London: Oxford University Press.

Winsor, Diana (1987) 'Small is educational', *The Sunday Times colour supplement*, 4 October, pp. 32–36.

Wober, Mallory (1971) *English Girls' Boarding Schools*, London: Allen Lane.

Woodfield, Sir R. (1987) *Efficiency Scrutiny of the Supervision of Charities. Report to the Home Secretary and the Economic Secretary to the Treasury*, London: HMSO.

Index

130

Index

Headmasters' Conference 4, 5–7,
    11, 22, 39, 40, 46–8, 51, 53,
    54, 56, 58, 114
higher education 48–52, 70, 81–4,
    86–7
Hillgate Group 93, 112
Hills, G. 82
historical development 15–18, 19–32
HM Forces 76
HMI 77
Honey, J. 4, 6, 7, 22
Hooper, Baroness 111
housing 62–3, 72
Humphrey, C. 98, 99

ideology 65–7
Incorporated Association of
    Preparatory Schools 9, 57, 58
Independent Schools' Association
    Incorporated 11, 51, 53, 57, 58
Independent Schools Information
    Service 4, 12
Independent Schools Joint Council
    4, 31
inequality 66, 105, 113, 116
Inner London Education Authority
    86, 98
Institute of Economic Affairs 82, 93

James, E. 118
Jewish schools 11, 13
John Loughborough School 13, 114
Johnson, D. 43
Jones, S. 90, 108, 116
Joseph, Sir K. 14, 78, 87
Jowell, R. 36
Judd, J. 77

Kilquhanity House 13
Kingshurst City Technology College
    90, 92
Kinnock, N. xi, 32, 77
Kirkman, S. 77

Labour Party 23, 25, 27, 29–34,
    37, 38, 52, 75, 103–4
Lamb, F. 8
Lambert, R. 7, 8, 29, 54
Lancing College 6

Lawlor, S. 96, 97
leadership 54
Leinster-Mackay, D. 5, 9, 20, 22
leisure 57
Lester, A. 119
local financial management 85,
    98–102, 107, 110–11, 119, 121
Lodge, B. 57
luck 121
MacDonald Fraser, G. 7
Mack, E.C. 7
magnet schools 90–1, 118, 120
McLean, M. 14
Maitland, N. 14
Manpower Services Commission 14
marketization 79–80
Marks, J. 93
Marlborough College 7, 22
Maychell, K. 79
Merchant Taylors' School 4, 22
meritocracy 41
Metz, M.H. 90
Millham, S. 7
Ministry of Defence 76
Mishra, R. 62
MORI 43–4, 97
Morrish, I. 20
mortgage relief 62
Mount St Mary's College 6
Murray, H. 82
Musgrave, P. 22

National Association of Head
    Teachers 95
national curriculum, 85, 119
National Health Service 64
National Society for Promoting the
    Education of the Poor 20
National Union of Teachers 95
nationalization 66, 106
Neill, A.S. 13
Netherlands, 117
Newcastle Commission 21–2
Newsom, J. 29
North London Collegiate School 8
Norwood Report 27

O'Connor, M. 76
Ogilvie, V. 7

132